Campaign • 108

OSPREY
PUBLISHING

Marathon 490 BC

The first Persian invasion of Greece

Nicholas Sekunda • Illustrated by Richard Hook

Series editor Lee Johnson • Consultant editor David G Chandler

First published in Great Britain in 2002 by Osprey Publishing,
Midland House, West Way, Botley, Oxford OX2 0PH, UK
443 Park Avenue South, New York, NY 10016, USA
Email: info@ospreypublishing.com

CIP Data for this publication is available from the British Library

ISBN 1 84176 000 5

Editor: Lee Johnson
Design: The Black Spot
Index by David Worthington
Maps by The Map Studio
3D bird's-eye views by The Black Spot
Battlescene artwork by Richard Hook

Originated by Magnet Harlequin, Uxbridge, UK
Printed in China through World Print Ltd.

05 06 07 08 09 10 9 8 7 6 5 4 3 2

For a catalogue of all books published by Osprey Military
and Aviation please contact:

NORTH AMERICA
Osprey Direct, 2427 Bond Street, University Park,
IL 60466, USA
E-mail: info@ospreydirectusa.com

ALL OTHER REGIONS
Osprey Direct UK, P.O. Box 140, Wellingborough,
Northants, NN8 2FA, UK
E-mail: info@ospreydirect.co.uk

www.ospreypublishing.com

Artist's note

Readers may care to note that the original paintings from
which the colour plates in this book were prepared are
available for private sale. All reproduction copyright
whatsoever is retained by the Publishers. All enquiries
should be addressed to:

Scorpio Gallery
PO Box 475,
Hailsham,
East Sussex
BN27 2SL
UK

The Publishers regret that they can enter into no
correspondence upon this matter.

Acknowledgements

As usual, first and foremost, I would like to thank Richard
Brzezinski for his moral support and immense practical
help rendered during the extremely difficult period writing
this book. If any general reader can understand anything of
what I try to say, this is entirely due to his help. I would also
like to thank Basil Petrakos, Honorary Ephor of Antiquities
for Attica, for his assistance obtaining illustrations and
reasearch materials, and Lee Johnson for his patience
during the writing of this book, which extended beyond any
conceivable deadline. Finally I would like to thank Dr.
Michael Vickers for his help and advice. All uncredited
images are from the author's collection.

KEY TO MILITARY SYMBOLS

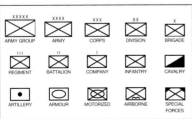

Marathon 490 BC

The first Persian invasion of Greece

CONTENTS

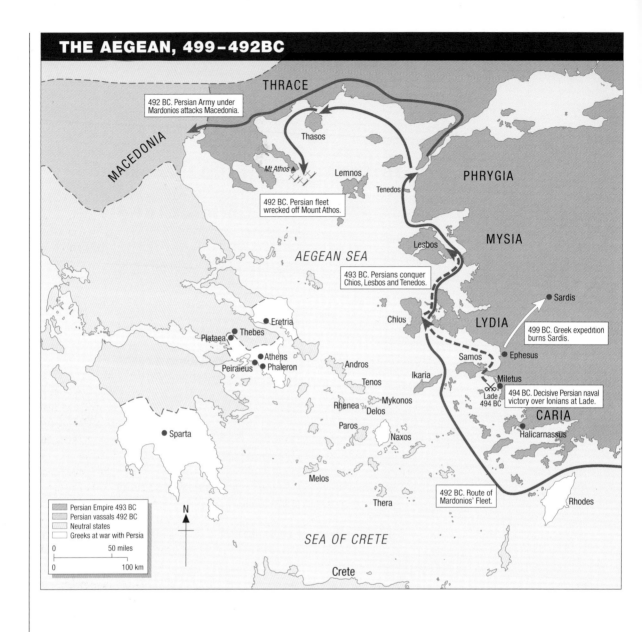

THE AEGEAN, 499–492BC

THRACE

492 BC. Persian Army under
Mardonios attacks Macedonia.

MACEDONIA

Thasos

Lemnos

Mt Athos

492 BC. Persian fleet
wrecked off Mount Athos.

Tenedos

PHRYGIA

MYSIA

AEGEAN SEA

Lesbos

493 BC. Persians conquer
Chios, Lesbos and Tenedos.

Sardis

Chios

499 BC. Greek expedition
burns Sardis.

LYDIA

Eretria

Plataea

Thebes

Andros

Samos

Ephesus

Athens

Peiraieus   Phaleron

Tenos

Ikaria

Miletus

494 BC. Decisive Persian naval
victory over Ionians at Lade.

Rhenea   Mykonos

Lade
494 BC

CARIA

Delos

Sparta

Paros

Naxos

Halicarnassus

Melos

492 BC. Route of
Mardonios' Fleet.

Rhodes

Thera

SEA OF CRETE

Persian Empire 493 BC
Persian vassals 492 BC
Neutral states
Greeks at war with Persia

N

0   50 miles
0   100 km

Crete

ORIGINS OF THE CAMPAIGN

The Persians attempted to invade mainland Greece twice – once in 490 and again in 480–479. These are conventionally called the First and Second Persian Wars. These terms are not entirely satisfactory, as they betray a Greek- and European-centred perspective. I would prefer to use the terms First and Second Persian invasions of Greece. The key battle of the first campaign was Marathon. Its strategic effect was limited, for it did nothing to prevent the second invasion which came a decade later. The moral effect was enormous. It was the first time a Greek army had successfully faced the Persian enemy and demonstrated the superiority of hoplite tactics and equipment.

Tyranny and democracy at Athens

At the time of Marathon, Athens had only recently emerged as a democracy from nearly half a century of government under the Peisistratid dynasty of 'tyrants'. The Greek definition of a tyrant does not have the connotations of modern usage. An absolute ruler, be he good or bad, who had established his rule through force was a tyrant, as opposed to a king, who ruled in accordance with natural custom.

Peisistratos first made himself tyrant around 561BC. His enemies succeeded in expelling him, but he returned in 546. Landing at Marathon, he defeated his enemies at Pallene and re-took Athens. After the death of Peisistratos from disease in 527 the tyranny was assumed by his two sons Hippias and Hipparchos. Conditions worsened as foreign dependencies were lost with the advance of Persia. In 514 Hipparchos was assassinated

The evidence from literary sources can to some extent be supplemented by representational evidence. The richest source is the 'Oxford Brygos cup', so-called because the potter Brygos has left his name painted on one of the handles. Although the date of production of the vase cannot be established with complete certainty, it seems likely to refer to the battle of Marathon.

Early depiction of the assassination of Hipparchos by Harmodios and Aristogeiton on a vase painted by the 'Copenhagen Painter'. It perhaps represents an early statue group on the Acropolis destroyed in the Persian sack of 480/79, and later replaced by a more dramatic composition designed by Kritios and Nesiotes in 477/76. (Langlotz, *Griechische Vasen in Würzburg* pl. 82)

by the 'tyrant-slayers' Harmodios and Aristogeiton. Hippias became increasingly apprehensive, and made an alliance to strengthen his position – giving his daughter away in marriage to Aiantides the son of Hippokles tyrant of Lampsakos, who had great influence with King Darius. Three years later Hippias was deposed by an invasion of the Lakedaimonian King Kleomenes and fled under truce to Sigeion, from there to Lampsakos, and then to the court of Darius. He had to wait a further 20 years before he returned to Attica, by then an old man, accompanied by a Persian army. Athens became a democracy and a new constitution was introduced by Kleisthenes in 508/07.

The Ionian Revolt, 499–494BC

The Persian Empire had reached the Aegean in 547BC and the local Greek cities had a new set of masters. During the reigns of Cyrus and Cambyses Persian imperial expansion was largely directed elsewhere, and it was only after Darius came to the throne in 521 that Persia again looked to the west. Darius left Susa to start a campaign against Scythia. He crossed the Bosphorus, and then the Danube, on bridges of boats. Darius was forced to retreat, spent the next year in Sardis and then returned to Susa, leaving his brother Artaphernes as satrap in Sardis. His generals Megabazos and then Otanes continued the gradual pacification of Europe south of Scythia.

In 508, increasingly threatened by pressure from Sparta, Athenian envoys entered negotiations with Artaphernes at Sardis. When the satrap

Detail from the Great Relief of Darius from Behistun in Iran, carved about 30 years before Marathon, when Darius first seized the throne. The king, holding a bow, stands at his natural height of 5ft 10ins. Behind him stands the commander of the Spearbearers, Gobryas, the second man in the Empire. (Photo: Claus Breede, West Asian Department, Royal Ontario Museum)

demanded earth and water the Athenian envoys obliged (Hdt. 5.73). We do not fully understand what these symbolic gifts represented in Achaemenid diplomacy: alliance, submission, hospitality? The Athenian envoys possibly misunderstood the depth of the obligations they had entered into, and their actions were later disavowed by the Athenian assembly. In 505 Hippias turned up at Sardis and Artaphernes ordered the Athenians to take him back (Hdt. 5.96). The Athenians refused and relations between Athens and the Persians deteriorated.

This is why Athens became involved in the Ionian Revolt, which brought about the first Persian invasion of Greece. The Ionian Revolt was led by Aristagoras tyrant of Miletus. Aristagoras sought support for the revolt in the states of mainland Greece. King Kleomenes of Sparta refused aid, as he was reluctant to become involved in a largely naval campaign. However, the Athenians agreed to send 20 triremes to help the Ionians, tempted by the prospect of plentiful booty. They were supported by 5 triremes sent by the Eretrians.

The fleet landed at Ephesus in 499, supported by Ionian and Milesian triremes. The expeditionary force marched on Sardis, the Persian administrative centre for their westernmost provinces, and occupied it, whereupon Artaphernes retired to the citadel. An isolated fire started by a Greek soldier spread and burnt the city to the ground with considerable loss of civilian life. The Athenians sailed home with no booty. Herodotus (5.101) does not convey the outrage the Persians surely felt over the incident. A campaign of revenge on the Athenians and Eretrians was now inevitable.

The Ionian Revolt was only suppressed following a decisive Persian naval victory at Lade in 494 and the destruction of the city of Miletus. The Persian fleet sailed along the eastern coast of the Aegean Sea, subduing, in turn, the islands of Chios, Lesbos and Tenedos, which it reached in 493. In the following year, 492, a large Persian force under Mardonios invaded Macedonia. Herodotus (6.43.4) believed that their ultimate goal was Athens and Eretria. The expedition was a combined land and naval operation, but was called off when half the fleet was lost in a storm off Mount Athos.

Darius sent heralds to the states of Greece in 491 (or possibly 492), demanding earth and water. The states reacted differently. Most of the islands and many mainland cities complied with the Persian request. The Athenians, says Herodotus (7.133), threw the envoys into a chasm, the *barathron*, used for executing serious criminals. It was Miltiades, says Pausanias (3.12.7), who was responsible for their death. The envoys sent to Sparta were thrown into a well 'to collect their own earth and water'. Here too, their murder was probably designed to unify the citizens against Persia by complicity in the crime (Sealey 18). Darius ordered the construction of warships and horse-transports (Hdt. 6.48-9) and prepared for war.

OPPOSING COMMANDERS

ATHENIAN COMMANDERS

The command structure of the Athenian army was constantly evolving during the first half of the 5th century. Its precise form in 490 is not fully understood.

The leader of the army, according to Aristotle's *Athenian Constitution*, was one of the three traditional principal magistrates or *archons* called the Polemarch (22.2). This office, he says (3.2), had come into being 'because some of the kings were not good soldiers'. According to Herodotus (6.109.2) at the time of Marathon the Polemarch was selected by lot rather than elected, although Aristotle (22.5) says that selection of the archons by lot was introduced only in 487/86. Aristotle is probably correct. After this date the role of the Polemarch diminished and he was soon relegated primarily to religious functions necessary for the army.

At the time of Marathon the Polemarch still had many duties aside from his religious functions. He led the army as it marched out of the city and took up the post of honour on the extreme right wing of the battle line. It is possible that, contrary to the impression created by Herodotus, the Polemarch still retained overall command over the board of *strategoi*. Herodotus may have deliberately sought to emphasize the role Miltiades played in the battle and minimize the role of Kallimachos.

The Athenian army had been restructured into ten tribal regiments of hoplites in 508/507. The command structure was reformed in 501/500 to conform with this change. From that date on, ten generals (*strategoi*) were elected, one from each tribe. In the later 5th century the strategoi became separated from command of the tribal regiments, and one of the ten was appointed as overall commander of any particular expeditionary force. At Marathon their primary role was still as commanders of the ten tribal regiments. They also met as a board of generals to take common command decisions.

Kallimachos of Aphidna held the post of Polemarch at Marathon. A monument from the Athenian Acropolis, destroyed in the later Persian sack of 480/79, appears to have been dedicated during his year of office. It consisted of a tall column supporting a winged female figure, either Iris (the female messenger of the gods) or Nike (the goddess of victory). The inscription is only partly preserved, but well enough to identify a Polemarch from Aphidna who fought bravely in battle.

This inscription helps us understand the role of Kallimachos in 490. According to one restoration of the inscription (see illustrations) Kallimachos had been victorious in the Panathenaic Games of 490

Fragment of a pot from Eleusis (1223) painted by Euthymides showing Iris, the rainbow, the fleeting but brilliant phenomenon in the sky, which vanishes as quickly as it appears, the swift messenger of the gods. She is identified by her wings and her messenger's wand or *kerykeion*. Though painted two decades before Marathon, it shows her popularity in late Archaic Athens, and gives an idea of the appearance of the crowning element of the Kallimachos Monument. (*Hesperia* 5, p.66, fig. 5)

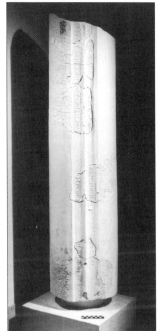

[Kallimachos] of Aphidn[a ded]icated [me] to Athena:
I am the mess[enger of the imm]ortals who have [their thrones on] O[lympos],
[because he was victorious, when he was Pole]march, in the festival of the Athenians.
And fighting mo[st bravely] of them all he won [fairest renown]
for Athenian men-at-arms and a mem[orial of his own valour].

before the battle was fought. The festival was celebrated on the 28th day of the month *Hekatombaion*, eight days or so before news of the Persian landing arrived at Athens. It may be that his victory was believed to have brought luck to the whole army. Other restorations of the inscription are possible. In one of them Kallimachos vows to erect the monument if he was victorious, apparently after making a personal vow to Iris.

One thing is certain. The column was an impressive monument erected by the Athenians to the honour of Kallimachos. It was sited on the Acropolis, overlooking the city, and was constructed shortly after the battle. At the same time Miltiades was dying in prison, fined 50 talents for deceiving the Athenian people. The picture we have of the relative roles played by Kallimachos and Miltiades may have been seriously distorted by the propaganda campaign mounted by Miltiades' son Kimon in the 460s to glorify the memory of his father. The monument is testimony in stone to the fact that the Athenians of 490 thought that Kallimachos had fought most bravely 'of them all', and he rather than Militiades had been the hero of the battle.

Miltiades was born in the late 550s, son of Kimon of the noble Philaid family, early opponents of the Peisistratid tyranny. Kimon left Athens and his brother, also Miltiades, established himself as ruler of the

The shaft of the Kallimachos monument (*IG* i^2 609; Athens, Epigraphic Museum 6339) has been reassembled from the debris of the Persian sack of 480/79. The difficulties of reading the inscription (drawing Helen Besi) are evident. The translation is of the restoration proposed by Harrison. The two surviving fragments of the female figure from the top (Athens, Epigraphic Museum 690) pose considerable problems of identification. Most favour Iris, but Harrison prefers Nike. The reference to 'the messenger of the immortals' suggests Iris. Reconstruction drawing after P. Lemerle *Bulletin de Correspondance Hellenique* 58 (1938) 443.

Thracian Chersonese along with a group of Athenian colonists. During his second period of rule, Peisistratos had succeeded in reconciling some of the noble families opposed to him, including the Philaids. Kimon returned to Athens, but lost his life in the power struggle following Peisistratos' death.

Kimon's son Miltiades continued to enjoy favour. He was appointed archon for the year 524/23, and about this time he married for the first time, possibly to a relative of Hippias. Around 516 Hippias sent Miltiades to rule in the Thracian Chersonese. This followed the death of Miltiades' brother, Stesagoras, who had earlier succeeded his childless uncle, the elder Miltiades.

Relations with Hippias became increasingly strained. Miltiades possibly divorced his first wife when Hippias gave his daughter away to Aiantides of Lampsakos. Lampsakos, on the opposite side of the Hellespont, was the arch-rival of the Thracian Chersonese. He took as his second wife Hegesipyle, daughter of the Thracian king Oloros. His son and heir Kimon was born about 510. Miltiades was obliged to seek an accommodation with the Persians, and accompanied Darius as a subject on his Scythian Campaign. Miltiades was left with the other Ionian commanders at the bridge of boats over the Danube. He later claimed to have recommended that the Greeks break up the bridge, leaving Darius stranded in Scythia, but this could be a later fabrication aimed at improving his image in Athens.

Miltiades became increasingly insecure. He sought rapprochement with the new democratic government in Athens and co-operated with the Athenians in seizing the island of Lemnos (possibly in 499). In 493, after the collapse of the Ionian Revolt, when the Persian fleet reached Tenedos, Miltiades fled for Athens. He succeeded in surviving a trial for tyranny, and re-entered Athenian political life. Metiochos, his son by his first marriage, was captured by the Phoenician fleet and never returned to Athens, but was granted a Persian wife and lands by Darius. The Persian kings liked to collect Greek noble exiles who could be put to work for them in the future.

Miltiades would have been in his early 60s when the battle of Marathon was fought. He had lived only a year or two in the new democratic Athens. It would be wrong to see him as a passionate defender either of liberty or democracy, as many ancient authors imply. Miltiades had no choice but to return and fight for Athens.

There are good reasons for thinking that the role Miltiades played in the victory is exaggerated in our sources at the expense of Kallimachos. Nevertheless, his service alongside the Persians in the Scythian campaign must have given insights into Persian methods of operation that were invaluable to the Athenians. Much of the credit for the Athenian victory must be due to the courage and determination of Miltiades, to save his own skin if nothing else.

Arimnestos commanded the Plataean contingent at Marathon. After the battle the Plataeans built a temple to Athena Areia 'the Warlike' in Plataea with their share of the spoils of the battle. At the feet of the cult

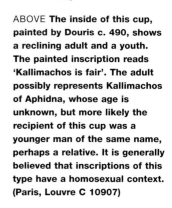

ABOVE **The inside of this cup, painted by Douris c. 490, shows a reclining adult and a youth. The painted inscription reads 'Kallimachos is fair'. The adult possibly represents Kallimachos of Aphidna, whose age is unknown, but more likely the recipient of this cup was a younger man of the same name, perhaps a relative. It is generally believed that inscriptions of this type have a homosexual context. (Paris, Louvre C 10907)**

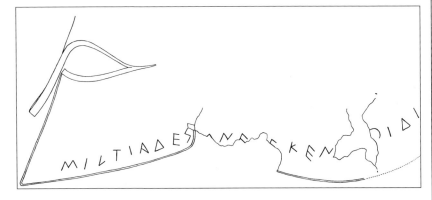

statue was a portrait of Arimnestos, who, according to Pausanias (9.4.2), commanded the Plataeans at the battle of Marathon and also at Plataea 11 years later. The fact that the same person held command in both crucial campaigns surely attests to the decisive role of Arimnestos in the politics of the small state. He may have been instrumental in the brave decision of this tiny city to stand by their Athenian allies. Many historians (Lazenby 10–11) believe he is the direct source for Herodotus' account (9.72) of the death of Kallikrates the Lakedaimonian at the battle of Plataea. It is possible that he also supplied Herodotus with information on Marathon.

PERSIAN COMMANDERS

The satrap was the king's representative in each satrapy, or province, of the Persian Empire. The key satrap of western Anatolia was **Artaphernes the Elder**, who was based at Sardis. It was Persian practice to separate military from administrative functions in the same area, though one individual could be both satrap in one region and military commander

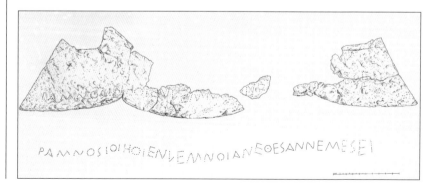

ABOVE **Remains of one of a number of statues from the Acropolis (606), destroyed by the Persians in 480, showing young Athenian aristocrats mounted**

TOP, LEFT **Attic plate (Oxford, Ashmolean Museum 310) by Paseas, about 515BC showing a youth, not yet wearing a beard as all adults did at this time, dressed and equipped as a Scythian mounted archer, and inscribed 'Miltiades is beautiful'. Wade-Gery (*Journal of Hellenic Studies* 1951) suggested it may show an equestrian statue of the young Miltiades dedicated earlier on the Acropolis, but the inscription probably refers to a younger relative of the general.**

LEFT **Corroded fragment of the left cheek-piece of a Corinthian helmet found in the sanctuary of Nemesis at Rhamnous. The inscription on the whole helmet (drawing K. Eliaki) states that 'The Rhamnousians dedicated [this, taken] on Lemnos, to Nemesis' as booty from Miltiades' expedition to Lemnos c. 499. It was dedicated by the deme-contigent from Rhamnous. (Archaeological Society at Athens)**

Fragment of a helmet dedicated on the Acropolis. The punch-dots preserve a few letters of an inscription (*IG* i₎ 453) which suggest that it had also been captured at Lemnos. Like most booty, this helmet was hammered onto the wooden beams of a temple: note the nail-hole bottom left. (Athens, National Museum 7322)

in another. Artaphernes, although responsible for security within his own satrapy, did not take command of the expedition. Nor did **King Darius** take personal command of the expedition. He had now been ruling for more than three decades. We do not know his age precisely, but he was to die shortly after the campaign in 486.

Datis was appointed to supreme command of the 490 invasion force in place of Mardonios, after the expedition in the northern Aegean had met with such ill-fortune in 493 (Hdt. 6.94). Very little is known about Datis. Both Herodotus (6.94) and Diodorus (10.27) state he was 'of Median race', but this may be a Greek misunderstanding of the Achaemenid practice of naming eminent Persians after the provinces they governed. In his *Moralia* (305B) Plutarch says that Datis was a satrap, information repeated in Suidas (*Hippias*). It seems probable that Datis was a Persian, holding the office of satrap of Media in parallel with a field command.

Datis is perhaps mentioned in a tablet from Persepolis written in Elamite (Lewis):

'7 *marris* beer Datiya received as rations. He carried a sealed document of the King. He went forth from Sardis (via) express (service), went to the King at Persepolis. 11th month, year 27. (At) Hidali.'

It is possible that 'Datiya' is the Datis of Greek texts. Few individuals mentioned in the Persepolis ration documents are issued with a ration as large as 70 quarts of wine or beer to distribute among their entourage, which means that Datiya was an extremely important official of the Empire. The tablet was issued between 17 January and 15 February 494 at Hidali, only three stations on the road from Persepolis. The date falls within the winter preceding the final campaign of the Ionian Revolt. He is travelling on the authorization of the king. Journeys were normally authorized at their point of origin, and so 'Datiya' would have been returning from a journey to Sardis on the orders of Darius. This could have been a tour of inspection and co-ordination for the final campaign. Datiya (Datis?) may therefore have held an earlier command in the west.

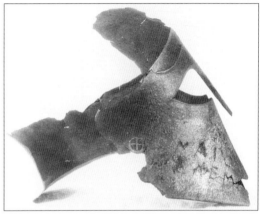

A relatively complete Corinthian helmet discovered during excavations at Olympia and published by Emil Kunze, *Festschrift C. Weikert* (Berlin 1955) 9–11. The inscription states it was captured on Lemnos and dedicated by the Athenians. (Athens, National Museum 15189)

Bringing these few scraps of information together, it seems that Datis was overall commander of all Persian forces in the West, superior in rank to all local satraps and other generals appointed by the king, perhaps both during the closing stages of the Ionian Revolt and throughout the Marathon campaign. Perhaps his title was 'Leader of the Hosts' – *kara-naya*.

Artaphernes the Younger is the only other Persian commander mentioned at Marathon. Herodotus (6.94-5) merely states that Datis and Artaphernes commanded the expedition, that they left the King's presence and went to Cilicia and took over the fleet assigned to each of them. This might lead one to believe that the two held equal commands, but it is evident that Datis held the supreme command. In a reference of much later date, Pausanias (1.32.7) mentions the 'mangers of the horses of Artaphernes' in the rocks at Marathon, which suggests that Artaphernes commanded the cavalry.

Artaphernes 'the Younger' was son of Artaphernes the Elder, previously mentioned, brother of Darius and satrap in Sardis. Herodotus distorts his name as Artaphrenes, while Ktesias calls his father Ataphernes. This is nearest to the Old Persian form of the name, Atrfarnah – 'with the majesty of the fire-god'.

Of Artaphernes the Younger we know very little. He first appears during the Marathon campaign. He may have already gained some experience of service in the west in the company of his father, or he may

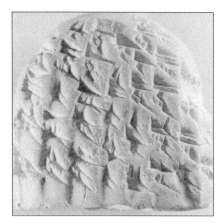

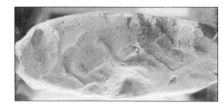

Fortification tablet excavated at Persepolis. The main body of text on the obverse mentions the return of Datiya (Datis?) to Persepolis from Sardis in 494. On the reverse is a small stamp seal bearing a figure at left facing an altar with an animal on it, with a moon above. This is Datiya's seal, or perhaps that of a guide acting for him. The left edge is stamped with a much simpler seal, which perhaps belonged to the ration supplier at Hidali. (University of Chicago, Oriental Institute, Q-1809)

have remained at court. Following the Marathon campaign he accompanied Datis back to Susa with the Eretrian prisoners (6.119). He later took part in the second Persian campaign against Greece in 480, commanding one of the army contingents (7.74).

OPPOSING ARMIES

THE ATHENIANS

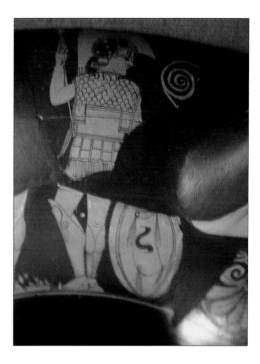

The Athenian army at Marathon was a wholly infantry force of hoplites.[1] It had been completely reorganized by Kleisthenes in 508/07. Previously different political factions at Athens had drawn support from three regions of Attica, known as 'Town', 'Shore' and 'Inland'. The Peisistratid tyrants had drawn much of their support from 'Inland', the mountainous areas of Attica. Kleisthenes' aim was to mix up contingents from different areas in a new military and political division called a 'tribe' (*phyle*). Kleisthenes sent a list of 100 heroes to Delphi, from which the Delphic priestess selected ten. Each of the new tribes was given the name of one of these heroes.

Each new tribe had three 'thirds' (*trittyes*) assigned to it by lot, one each from 'Town', 'Shore' and 'Inland' areas. There were a total of 30 trittyes, ten located in the 'Town', ten in the 'Shore', and ten in the 'Inland'. Each *trittys* was of about the same size, and fielded a company, or *lochos*, of 300 hoplites commanded by a *lochagos*.

Attica was divided into more than 100 'parishes', each known as a 'deme' (*demos*) with a *demarchos* at its head. Parish registers listing its citizens formed the basic documentation for elections and for military mobilization. An Athenian citizen remained liable for military service outside the borders of Attica until the age of 50. In times of national danger all males capable of bearing arms were pressed into service. Neighbouring demes were grouped together into trittyes. The number of demes in a trittys varied. For example the trittys of Acharnai, a large town lying outside the city of Athens, was formed of a single deme, also called Acharnai.

Kleisthenes expanded the military strength of Athens by admitting to citizenship free foreigners resident in Attica, and freed slaves. They would have been enrolled in the numerically weaker demes, balancing them to achieve a strength of 300 for each trittys and a total strength of 9,000 for the army as a whole.

Over the 17 years between the reforms of Kleisthenes and the battle of Marathon the balance of the strength of these administrative divisions may have shifted. The number of citizens becoming too old for service would rarely match the number of younger citizens coming of age, and the overall size of the army might fluctuate up and down from 9,000.

Armour typically worn by contemporary Athenian warriors is shown in this back view, a detail from the Oxford Brygos cup. Plate armour has been completely replaced by composite constructions. This is shown most clearly in the shoulder-pieces: the scales laid running upwards, not downwards as was more normal. Note the square nape-protector, an extension of the back-plate of the shoulder-pieces. The skull of the helmet is of an extremely interesting and rare construction. It also seems to be a composite construction of plates or scales covered in leather. The lighter spots visible probably represent the ends of rivets holding them together. Greaves and a hoplite shield and spear complete the panoply. The scene is most plausibly interpreted as showing the veterans of Marathon arming themselves to defend their homeland again.

1 See Warrior 27, *Greek Hoplite*, N. Sekunda (Osprey 2000).

Further details of contemporary Athenian hoplite weaponry: to the right, a back view of the thin, springy bronze greaves. Both hoplite shields have the bronze rims typical of hoplite shields, but the round bowls display unusual features. The one lying flat is decorated in a diamond-pattern, presumably either painted directly onto the bronze surface, or onto a leather cover glued onto the latter. It would, however, be difficult to understand the patterning on the bowl of the second shield as showing anything other than scales. In such case it may be that in the very first decades of the 5th century the hoplite shield was sometimes of composite construction too.

Pausanias (7.15.7) states that Miltiades and the Athenians set slaves free before the battle of Marathon. Later (10.20.2) he notes that no more than 9,000 Athenians marched to Marathon 'including the old and slaves'. It seems that the army had fallen significantly from its establishment strength, even after 'old men' over 50 had been mobilized. Miltiades therefore persuaded the Athenian assembly to move the necessary legislation to free the number of slaves necessary to bring the army up to full strength. Hammond (1992, 147–50) has suggested that the slaves fought in a separate unit. But, in view of the earlier practice, it is more probable that they were integrated into the tribal regiments to bring them up to strength.

THE PLATAEANS

The small Boeotian city of Plataea, which bordered Attica, had been allied to Athens for three decades before Marathon. Plataea sought Athenian protection against Thebes, the most important city of the region, and the Thebans' long term policy of bringing the whole of Boeotia under their power. Herodotus does not record the strength of the Plataean contingent, but he (6.108.1) does state that they sent a full levy (*pandemei*). Justin (2.9) and Nepos (*Milt.* 5) say the Plateans numbered 1,000 hoplites. Strangely, when fighting against the Persians 11 years later in 479 Herodotus gives their number as 600 (Hdt. 9.28). It may be that some of the Plataeans had gone over to the Persian camp, as had happened in most other Boeotian states. A Plataean strength of 1,000 at Marathon seems reasonable.

Pausanias (1.32.3) reports a grave of the Plataeans and slaves at Marathon, though some modern historians have doubted that Plataean citizens and Athenian slaves would have been buried together. Van Der Veer (303) suggests that as 'non-Athenians' they could have been. We do not know whether the slaves had been given freedom before the battle, or only promised the reward of it after, in which case the fallen would have died unfree. Even if freed before the battle, this does not mean they automatically received Athenian citizenship.

Marinatos believed the 'Classical' tumulus at Vrana to be the tomb of the Plataeans. The stone entrance at the front is modern and allows viewing of the burials in the centre of the tumulus, which were not filled in after excavation.

In 1970 Spyridon Marinatos identified an impressive tumulus over 3m high and 30m in diameter, as the tomb of the Plataeans, even though it lies at Vrana, 2.5km from the Sorós. This identification has obvious problems, not least that Pausanias implies it lay close to the tomb of the Athenians, which can certainly be identified with the Sorós (Welwei, *Historia* 28 (1979) 101–6). If the graves do not belong to the Plataeans and Athenian slaves, their date and the fact that a monumental tumulus was raised over them, indicates a connection with the battle (Van Der Veer 304).

THE PERSIANS

Herodotus gives no figures for the strength of the Persian forces at the battle, and indeed there is no reason why the Greeks should have had an accurate idea of the enemy strength. Within little more than 10 years the Athenians were claiming to have defeated 46 nations at Marathon (Hdt. 9.27.5). In the absence of fact, later authors wildly exaggerate Persian numbers. The Roman writer Ampelius (5.9) puts the number of troops commanded by Datis (and Tissaphernes!) at 80,000. Simonides, in an epigram commissioned by the Athenians to commemorate the battle, put the Persian strength at 90,000, a figure which Hammond (1968, 33) thought to be 'within the scope of reason'. According to Nepos (*Milt.* 4) Datis commanded a total force of 200,000 infantry, of which 100,000 fought at the battle, while Artaphernes commanded 10,000 horse and the fleet numbered 500 ships. In his *Moralia* (305 b) Plutarch puts the Persian strength at 300,000, a figure repeated in Pausanias (4.25.5) and Suidas (*Hippias* 2). Plato (*Menexenos* 240 A) says Datis was given 500,000 men in 300 ships – a physical impossibility. Lysias (2.21) also quotes 500,000 men, while Justin (2.9) increases this to 600,000.

The 'Classical' tumulus covered 11 burials: nine males aged 20 to 30, a boy aged about ten, and a male about 40. Marinatos suggested that the boy might have been a messenger employed to relay orders. The nine inhumations are marked 1 to 9 and the two cremations A and B. The graves had stone markers erected over them. Lightly incised on the stone over the grave of the older man was the name Archias. Marinatos assumed Archias was a Plataean officer, but the letters are in the Attic alphabet not the Boeotian. The tumulus, of river pebbles, was probably heaped over these marked graves at a later date. The skeleton and skull in burial number 4 were one of the best preserved of the burials in the tumulus. It could be the final resting place of one of the Plataeans killed at Marathon. The grave goods were very poor. The pottery dates to 500–490 and includes this Attic black-figure plate (Marathon Museum K 156). It shows two running hoplites, who are wearing Corinthian helmets and, unusually, cloaks. (Archaeological Society at Athens)

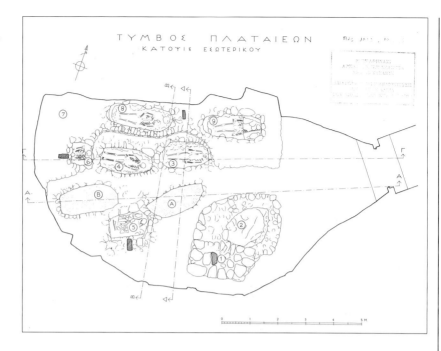

Two later examples of *spara* shields discovered during excavations at Dura-Europos. The complete example is in Damascus (122), the fragmentary one in New Haven (1929.417). The *spara* was constructed by flexing osiers of one colour through geometrically arranged holes in a rectangle of rawhide dyed a different colour. As the rawhide dried and flexed the osiers, the shield took on great resilience and springiness. Note also the handle, which would have been attached to the centre of the shield. (Yale University Art Gallery, Dura-Europos Collection 1933).

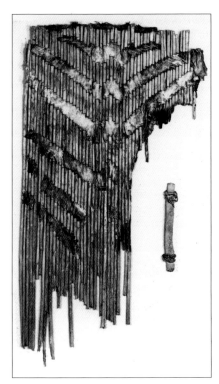

Our starting point for an estimate of Persian strength must be Herodotus' statement (6.95) that the fleet numbered 600 triremes. This figure of 600 seems to be a standard strength for the mobilized Persian fleet. The fleets raised for the Scythian campaign (4.87.1) and for the battle of Lade (6.9.1) were both of this strength, as were many Persian fleets mobilized during the 4th century. We know that if a trireme was fully manned with rowers it could carry a maximum of about 200 men – 170 rowers and 30 others. So the absolute maximum number of humans the fleet could physically have transported was 120,000. Troop-carrying triremes had a reduced complement of rowers – 60 has been suggested for Datis' fleet by comparison with contemporary practice (H.T. Wallingha, *Ships & Sea-Power before the Great Persian War* (1993) 184). In

Grace H. Macurdy published this Attic white-ground *lekythos*, 'probably made not long after the battle of Marathon' and perhaps showing it. The fallen Persian is armed with a kopis-type sword, the sheath for which is shown slung at his left side. Macurdy interpreted the striped object under the hoplite's shield as the Persian's *spara*, but it might be a hoplite shield-apron. She also thought the Persian is wearing gold anklets as a badge of rank, but it could be the edges of his trousers. The trees in the background may be an artistic convention rather than a representation of the sacred grove of Marathon (*American Journal of Archaeology* 36 (1932) 27).

RIGHT **A Persian *sparabara* from the Oxford Brygos cup, shown at the moment in the battle when the Greek hoplite charge meets the Persian shield-wall.**

ABOVE **Second Persian soldier from the Oxford Brygos cup. His cuirass is partially covered in decorated leather and the side plates and shoulder plates are made of bronze scales.**

BELOW, RIGHT **This Persian struck down by the charging hoplite, also from the Oxford Brygos cup, wears a composite cuirass, identical to those used by the Greeks.**

the event of a naval battle, these reduced crews could be consolidated into a smaller number of fully manned fighting triremes.

The aim of the expedition was to enslave the populations of Eretria and Athens – tens of thousands of people – and to bring them before Darius, so space would have to be made for this human cargo on the way home. Similarly, the requirement of storage space for supplies on the way out meant that the ships could not have been loaded to their maximum capacity with fighting men.

Herodotus (7.184) records that during Xerxes' invasion of Greece each trireme carried 30 Persians, Medes or Sakai. This is the standard number of fighting men we would expect to travel in a Persian or Greek trireme. Chiot triremes carried the maximum number recorded, 40, at the battle of Lade (Hdt. 6.15.1). This would give a total number of either 18,000 or 24,000 men. Lazenby (46) reaches the second figure by the same reasoning; other historians have arrived at similar figures by different methods. Hammond (1968, 32) suggested that the Persians

Two views of Persian *arstibara* 'spear-bearers' from Persepolis. Unlike the archers shooting from behind the cover of the shields of the *sparabara*, the *arstibara* put most reliance on their spears. The Persians in the centre of the line at Marathon may have been armed in this way. Note the 'scallops' in the side of their shields. (Michael Roaf)

must have numbered a minimum of 25,000 fighting troops, as they potentially faced the 20,000-plus hoplites that Eretria, Athens and Sparta were together capable of fielding.

The Persian army was organized into 'thousands' *hazarabam* of 1,000 men and 'myriads' *baivarabam* of 10,000 men. I suggest that the main force of infantry at Marathon consisted of two *baivarabam*. If Datis did indeed hold the office of satrap of Media, these troops may have been recruited in Media. Certainly Ktesias (18) says that the fleet commanded by Datis was 'Median', though Greek sources often use this word as a synonym for Persian.

These troops would have been archers shooting from behind a wall of pavise-like shields (*spara*), held by troops known as *sparabara* in Old Persian and *gerrhophoroi* in Greek. In addition a few *hazarabam* of élite infantry may have been present: Herodotus (6.113) mentions that at the battle the centre was held by the best troops: the Persians themselves and the Sakai. These 'Persians' are likely to have been a *hazarabam* of spearbearers (*arstibara*). It was standard practice for senior commanders to be accompanied by a bodyguard of such troops. There were presumably two or three *hazarabam* of Sakai.

The fleet also carried a number of Aeolian and Ionian soldiers, though these seem to have taken no part in the action.

Also present was a cavalry contingent. Herodotus (6. 95) mentions the Persian horse-transports separately from the rest of the fleet assigned to Datis and Artaphernes. The number of transports is uncertain. Given that Athens, Eretria and Sparta had no effective force of cavalry at this date, even a modest number of cavalry would have ensured Persian superiority in this arm. For numbers we are again reduced to guesswork. Hippias would have known that 1,000 Thessalian cavalry had been sufficient to deal with the Athenian army in 511 (Hammond 1968, 44). My guess is that the expedition disposed of either one *hazarabam* of 1,000 cavalry, or two: one for each wing of the army. Thucydides (6. 43) states that the Athenians sent a trireme carrying 30 horses with the fleet to Sicily in 413BC, which suggest that 2,000 horses required about 70 triremes. The riders presumably sailed in the same ships as their steeds. This was presumably the fleet assigned separately to Artaphernes.

The Oxford Brygos cup (Barrett & Vickers) contains a wealth of pictorial information concerning the troops fighting on the Persian side at Marathon, perhaps from personal observation by the artist, or from sketches made of the equipment and clothing of the dead. We know that Persians, Sakai, and other nationalities were fighting at Marathon, so it is impossible to establish the ethnic identity of the figures on the cup.

They wear sleeved tunics and trousers, made of leather or felt, highly decorated with applied bands of material in different colours. The sleeves generally have a ribbon of material stitched to the forward and rear seam. The rest of the sleeve is then decorated with bands of material stitched onto it, either horizontally in wavy or straight bands, or vertically in stripes. Sometimes the two sleeves are decorated differently, sometimes the same. The sleeves are finished off with a little roll at the cuff.

Trousers are decorated similarly. A dark coloured band of material runs up the front and back of each leg, presumably running along a seam. Sometimes the band of material runs along the outside of the leg, like piping along the seams of 19th-century military trousers. The areas of trouser demarcated by these vertical seams are sometimes left plain, and sometimes decorated by sewn-on horizontal bands, either wavy or straight.

The Persian hood with five lappets shown on the *sparabara* on p.23 (top) is non-standard in Greek art, suggesting the artist follows sources specific for Marathon. The cuirass is also non-standard. The small dots in the centre of the lozenges of the composite cuirass could be rivets holding bronze plates between surface layers of leather on the inside and outside of the cuirass; the diagonal lines may represent stitching. This is the Achaemenid equivalent of a medieval 'jack' or 'brigantine'. A line of *pteruges*, or groin-flaps, is attached at the bottom. These seem to be of stiff leather, deliberately split into 'tassels' at the bottom to prevent them chaffing the thighs. The trousers are decorated with stitched appliqué patches of darker coloured material in a diamond or irregular leaf-shape pattern. The boots are tied by wrapping flaps of leather around the ankle. These would end in lace-type thongs, which would be knotted somewhat higher up the ankle. The knot is obscured by the trousers. The boots would probably be of an undyed tan colour, though surviving paintings show Persian boots dyed yellow, red or even blue.

A second Persian soldier from the Oxford Brygos cup is shown on p.23 (top left). The breast section of his cuirass is covered with a layer of leather decorated with a lozenge pattern. Both side plates are shown, made of bronze scales sewn onto a stiff base and left uncovered. The shoulder plates are also made of bronze scales with rounded ends, bound at the edge with a leather band. The groin-flaps are rectangular metal plates with curved ends of the normal type, but covered with leather, painted half white and half black with a diagonal border. Under the groin-flaps he wears a garment which seems to be an apron of pleated material wrapped around the groin for extra protection, rather that a tunic. It is decorated with a single dark line running parallel to the edge.

A third Persian shown in the lower picture on p.23 falls beneath the charge of a Greek hoplite. The bottom of a bull's head is visible on the hoplite shield in the centre of the fragment. Beneath the hoplite shield is the *spara* (shield) of the Persian. The cuirass is identical to the type of composite cuirass used by Greeks. Just visible is an apron wrapped round his waist under the groin-flaps. Note the fine beard. On the left of the fragment the right forearm holds a *kopis* sword, of which the pommel is just visible. The *kopis* swords were rather like machetes in appearance, with iron blades slightly curving towards the tip on the outside, without guards, and with a handle consisting of two plates of wood or stone fixed to either side of the iron blade. They would be held in a scabbard of two wooden boards fixed together and covered in leather. Scabbards are often omitted from painted Greek vases.

OPPOSING PLANS

Portrait bust of Herodotus found in the Egyptian city of Athritis, a copy of an early 4th-century original. Herodotus is shown in early middle-age with a high, intelligent forehead and penetrating, critical gaze: most appropriate for 'the father of history' as Cicero called him. (New York, Metropolitan Museum 91.9, gift of George F. Baker in 1891)

The Persian objectives are not at all obvious. Our sources are too intimately tied up with Athenian issues to see the wider picture. One source reported in Suidas (*Hippias*) would have us believe that Hippias, the former tyrant of Athens, managed to persuade Darius to launch the expedition because the king had a penchant for Attic figs.

Herodotus (6.94) states that the task given by Darius to the Persian commanders was to enslave Athens and Eretria and to bring the slaves before him. This is confirmed by Plato (*Menexenus* 240B), who also states that Datis was ordered on pain of death to bring the Athenians and Eretrians as captives before him.

Plutarch (*Arist.* 5.1) says that the true aim of Darius was not just to punish the Athenians for burning Sardis, but to subdue all of Greece. This view is supported by Sealey (1976, 17). In 492/91 Persian envoys were sent to demand the submission of many Greek city-states besides Athens and Eretria. Sealey believes the expedition of 490 was intended 'to secure Eretria and Athens as bases for disembarking a larger force, which would follow later with the task of conquest'.

Even before the Scythian Expedition Darius had sent a party of 15 Persians to Greek lands, guided by Demokedes of Kroton, a doctor at the Persian court. This demonstrates that Darius' interests had a much wider range than Athens or Eretria a couple of decades or more before the Marathon campaign. They sailed from Sidon as far as the Greek cities in Italy, making observations of the shoreline as they travelled. These observations may have taken the form of sketches or notes written down by accompanying scribes. The group was shipwrecked in Italy and enslaved, but were redeemed and brought back to Darius.

In 501, at the beginning of the train of events which triggered off the Ionian Revolt, Aristagoras tyrant of Miletus had pointed out that Euboea could easily be attacked via Naxos, Paros, Andros and the other islands of the Cyclades (Hdt. 5.31). In the event the expedition got no further than Naxos, but the plan, which had been passed to Darius for approval, was doubtless remembered. After the suppression of the Ionian Revolt, Persian armed forces had steadily advanced west along the northern Aegean coast as far as Macedonia. But the wrecking of half the Persian fleet off Mount Athos appears to have given Darius second thoughts. In 490 the Cyclades route would be tried again.

The Persians were very aware of the concept that war is an extension of politics by other means. Their preferred method was to win without fighting, and they appear to have carried no siege equipment with them. If at all possible Athens and Eretria were to be captured by political intrigue. Hippias would have been in secret contact with his supporters at Athens, above all with the wealthy and numerous Alkmaeonid clan, and he perhaps guaranteed that he could bring the city over to the Persians.

Should fighting be necessary, the Persians realized that their greatest advantage lay in their superior cavalry. This is why Darius ordered the construction of horse-transports. These vessels did, however impose limitations on the fleet's activity. Amphibious operations, like night operations, are risky. Ideally the expeditionary force needed to land unopposed at a stretch of beach, where they could unload their horses, troops and stores with minimal danger to the ships, next to an anchorage protected from storms. The beach needed to back onto an open plain large enough for the cavalry to operate to best effect, close to a source of water for men and horses.

On the island of Euboea, the best landing beach was the Lelantine Plain between Chalcis and Eretria. In Attica there was more choice. Plains suitable for cavalry existed near Athens, for example the Thriasian Plain opposite Salamis and the plain between Phaleron and Athens. While a landing at either location would place the invasion force nearer their ultimate objective – Athens – the protracted process of disembarkation would almost certainly be opposed. At Marathon the Persian forces could be disembarked safely (Whatley 138). Recently the Bay of Loutsa has been suggested as another suitable point of disembarkation (Hodge 2001).

The fact that the Persians (on the advice of Hippias) decided to disembark at Marathon indicates that their operational aim was to draw the Athenian army out of Athens. They perhaps hoped that in the absence of the Athenian hoplites their political allies in the city could seize power and betray the city to them (Munro 1899).

Eretria and Athens decided to resist Persia, and Sparta declared its intention of supporting them. Sparta had built up a position of hegemony in Greece, and wished to maintain it at all costs. Failure to support either state would weaken the strength of her alliance, and their defeat would bring the Persians, the only alternative powerbase for an alliance of Greek states, onto Sparta's doorstep.

Once this political decision was taken, the military courses of action open to the Greek allies were limited. The first possibility was a pre-emptive strike on Persian dominions. But Sparta's policy was not to send forces by sea across the Aegean, a principle that had been in place since Sparta's failure to overthrow the tyrant Polykrates of Samos with a naval expedition in 526. In line with this policy King Kleomenes of Sparta had refused to send help to Aristagoras of Miletus during the Ionian Revolt. Consequently strategic initiative was sacrificed to the Persians. The Greeks were going to have to wait and react to Persian moves. This led to internal dissention in both Eretria and Athens as to how to react to the Persians when they did land.

THE CAMPAIGN

After leaving Darius, the Persian generals marched to the Aleian plain in Cilicia along with the army and camped there. There they were joined by, as Herodotus (6.95) puts it, 'the whole fleet assigned to each of the generals'. The majority of the fleet had probably been supplied by the Phoenician cities (Hdt. 6.118). The horses were loadcd aboard the transports, the army embarked, and the whole fleet set sail for Ionia.

THE CAMPAIGN IN THE CYCLADES

The first destination of the fleet may have been Rhodes. Before the unification of the island and the founding of the city of Rhodes, Lindos was the island's largest city. The presence of the Persian fleet near Rhodes is recorded in an inscription known as the *Lindian Chronicle*, which records the mythological history of the Sanctuary of Athena at Lindos (M.Hadas, *Hellenistic Culture* (1959) 166-7):

When Darius, King of Persia, sent forth a great army for the purpose of enslaving Hellas, this island was the first which his fleet visited. The people of the country were terrified at the approach of the Persians and fled for safety to all the strongholds, most of them gathering at Lindos. Thereupon the barbarians set about to besiege them, until the Lindians, sore-pressed by a water shortage, were minded to hand over the city to the enemy. Right at this juncture the goddess stood over one of the magistrates in his sleep and bade him be of good courage, since she herself would procure, by intercession with her father, the water they needed. The one who saw the vision rehearsed to the citizens Athena's command. So they investigated and found that they had only enough water to last five days, and accordingly they asked the barbarians for a truce for just that number of days, saying that Athena had sent to her father for help, and that if help did not come in the specified time they would surrender the city.

When Datis, the admiral of Darius, heard this request, he immediately burst out laughing. But the next day, when a great cloud gathered about the Acropolis and a heavy shower fell inside the cloud, so that contrary to all expectations the besieged had plenty of water, while the Persian army suffered for lack of it, the barbarian was struck by the epiphany of the goddess. He took off his personal adornment and sent it as an offering – his mantle, his necklace, and his bracelets, and in addition his tiara, his scimitar, and even his chariot.

As for Datis, he set forth on the business before him, after establishing peace with the besieged and declaring publicly, 'These men are protected by the gods.'

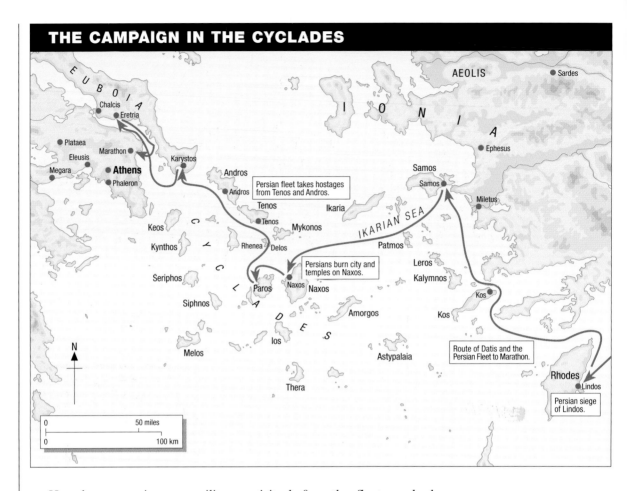

Herodotus mentions no military activity before the fleet reached Ionia, and this has led scholars to place the siege of Lindos, if not entirely fictitous, in the final campaign of the Ionian Revolt in 494 (Burn 1984, 210-1, 218). I believe, however, that the siege took place during the campaign of 490, and is but one of a number of omissions in Herodotus' account.

The fleet next sailed to Samos and then Eretria, straight across the Ikarian Sea. Herodotus (6.95) believes they took this route to avoid the dangerous waters off Mt. Athos, and also to bring the island of Naxos into their power. Ten years earlier the Naxians had successfully withstood a four-month siege by a Persian fleet of 200 ships. This time, says Herodotus, the Naxians fled for the hills. The Persians enslaved any Naxians they caught and burned their city and temples. Plutarch (*Mor.* 869B) has a different account, stating that, according to the Naxian chroniclers, Datis was driven off after burning the temples of Naxos, though he had not attempted to do any harm to the Naxians.

The Persians may have visited Paros next, for Herodotus (6.133) notes that Parians served the Persians at Marathon with their ships. Pausanias (1.33.2-3) records a tradition that the Persians, over-confident of success, took a block of Parian marble from which to carve a victory trophy. The Persian defeat was supposedly inflicted by the goddess Nemesis 'Retribution', who had a sanctuary at Rhamnous close by Marathon, as punishment for Persian presumption. According to

Pausanias Pheidias later carved a statue to Nemesis out of this very block of marble, captured after the battle.

The Delians fled to Tenos when the Persian fleet drew near. Datis respected the sanctity of Delos, anchoring off the neighbouring island of Rheneia. He sent a herald and explained that he had been ordered by Darius to do no harm to the island and its inhabitants out of respect to the twin gods, Apollo and Artemis, born on the island. He sacrificed 300 talents weight of frankincense on the altar, probably to satisfy the religious sensitivities of the Ionians serving in the expedition (Grote 258). When he sailed away from Delos the island was shaken by an earthquake. The Delians told Herodotus that this was the only earthquake ever recorded on Delos. Herodotus suggests it was a portent of troubles to come.

THE FALL OF ERETRIA

Datis continued towards Eretria, 'bringing with him Ionians and Aeolians' (Hdt. 6.98). Aeolis lies to the north of Ionia and was not visited by the fleet. Perhaps the Aeolians had joined Datis at Samos. Some of the Ionians may have been enslaved Naxians. Herodotus (6.99) states that some were the sons of the islanders living between Delos and Eretria, taken aboard the ships, as soldiers or hostages. These islands, Tenos and Andros and perhaps others, had not been subject to Persian rule previously. The aim was not to punish them as rebels, but rather to accept their submission as future tributary states of the Empire and levy a military contingent.

Arriving at Euboea the fleet put in at Karystos and likewise demanded hostages and soldiers. At first the Karystians refused, claiming they would not serve against their neighbours Athens and Eretria. The Persians besieged the Karystians and devastated their lands until they came over to the Persian side.

General Sir Frederick Maurice (19) observed: 'The choice of the bay of Karystos as an advanced base shows that the Persian commanders knew their business. It provided good shelter for the whole fleet and supplies of fresh water and food, and it was so placed as to be equally suitable for an attack either upon Athens or Ereteria, so its occupation gave no indication to the Greeks of the next Persian move.'

We are told the Eretrians sent to the Athenians for help: they may have sent to the Lakedaimonians too. The Athenians offered the help of their colonists settled on land near the Eretrian border seized from Chalkis in 506. Herodotus (5.77, 6.100) claims the colonists numbered 4,000, but this seems impossibly large (Berthold 86 n.16). According to Aelian (*VH* 7.1) they numbered 2,000.

Plato (*Menexenus* 240B) states that the Eretrians were among the most famous warriors in Greece, and by no means few in number. By 490 their number would have risen greatly above the 3,000 hoplites, 600 horse and 60 chariots that had once taken part in Eretrian festival processions (Strabo 10.1.10). Despite their numbers, the Eretrians were unable to form a coherent plan. Some were for abandoning the city and fleeing into the hills; others were willing to surrender the city. According to Herodotus (6.100) one of the Eretrian leaders, Aeschines son of

Plato preserves valuable details concerning the fall of Eretria which are at variance with the account of Herodotus. He also states that the Spartans were late in coming to the help of the Athenians because they were engaged in the suppression of a Messenian revolt. This portrait is reconstructed from a number of Roman marble busts, which are probably derived from two different contemporary portraits. (G.R. Levy, *Plato in Sicily* (1956) frontispiece)

Nothon, warned the Athenians of the situation, and urged them to consider the defence of Attica first. So the Athenian colonists left their Euboean settlements, crossed over the Straits to Oropus, and marched to Athens to join the main Athenian force.

The Persians secured Tamynai, Choireai and Aigilia in Eretrian territory. According to Whatley (138) these three potential landing points were seized so the Persians would be sure of having at least one beach where they could disembark unopposed. The Persians then successfully deployed their cavalry into the Lelantine plain and prepared to attack the enemy. The Eretrians refused to give battle, relying on the security of their city walls.

The Persian attack on Eretria lasted six days, and there were many casualties on both sides. On the seventh day Euphorbos son of Alcimachus and Philagros son of Kyneas, two prominent Eretrians (cf. Paus. 7.10.2), betrayed the city in return for Persian promises of land (Plut., *Mor.* 510B). It is possible that another Eretrian, Gongylos, accompanied Datis in order to liase with Eretrians willing to betray the city, as Hippias did at Athens (Avery 1972, 17). Xenophon (*Hell.* 3.1.6) reports that Gongylos had been the only Eretrian to support Persia, for which he was banished. He was given the Aeolian cities of Gambrion, Palaigambrion, Myrina and Gryneion by the Persian king, which his descendants were living in some 100 years later. However, Grote (259 n.2) notes that Plato makes no mention of any treachery in Eretria.

According to Herodotus the Persians entered Eretria, enslaved the inhabitants and plundered and burned the temples in retaliation for the temples burned at Sardis. Plato (*Menexenus* 240B–C) also has a somewhat different version of events. According to him resistance lasted three days, after which Datis made a thorough search of the countryside. His soldiers marched to the border of Eretria and made a line from sea

General view of Megalo-Mati. The ancient springs of Makaria which fed the Great Marsh lay here, where the rocky spur of the modern Stavrokoraki mountain reaches into the plain. This lay within the ancient deme of Trikorythos.

to sea, linked hands and traversed the whole of the country, so that they could report to the king with confidence, that no Eretrian had escaped them. Herodotus does not mention this 'netting' of Eretrian territory; while Strabo (10.1.10) incorrectly states that it was Herodotus, not Plato, who mentioned the 'netting' operation.

In a second work, the *Laws* (3.699D), Plato gives a slightly different account. He states that Datis sent to Athens an account of how not a man of the Eretrians had escaped him, and that this account 'whether true, or whatever its origin' struck terror into the Greeks generally, and especially the Athenians.

If the Persians did 'net' Eretria it would have been for propaganda effect with the intention of frightening the Athenians into submission. Nevertheless, enough Eretrians survived to man seven triremes at the battle of Salamis some ten years later (Hdt. 8.1, 46) and the Eretrians and their neighbours the Styreans supplied 600 hoplites for the Plataean campaign (Hdt. 9.28).

THE LANDING AT MARATHON

The present-day drained bed of the Stomi lake as viewed from cape Kynosoura. In the immediate foreground the sandy Schoinias beach, then a belt of umbrella pines. The light grassy area between these trees and the Drakonera mountain behind marks the area of the former lake.

After a few days on Euboea, Datis sailed for Attica. According to Herodotus (6.102) it was Hippias who guided the Persians to Marathon, as the most suitable spot for cavalry action and the nearest to Eretria. The night before the fleet sailed Hippias had a dream that he was lying with his own mother, which he interpreted to mean that he would return to Athens, and, having re-established his rule there, would die in his home country as an old man (Hdt. 6.107). On the way to Marathon the Persians disembarked the enslaved Eretrians on the island of Aigilia, which belonged to Styrea.

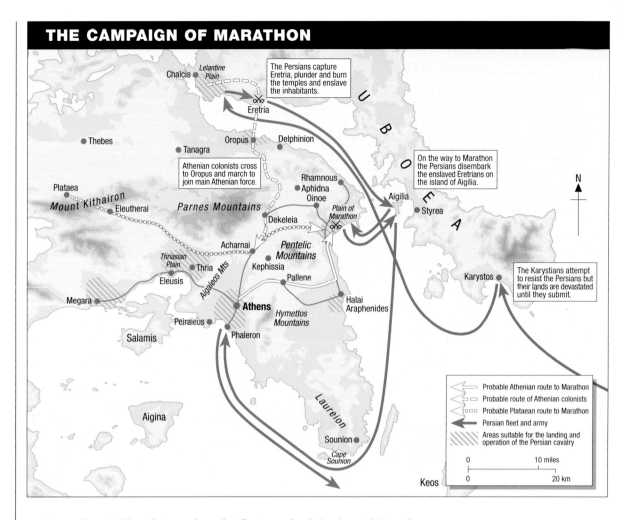

The Persians capture Eretria, plunder and burn the temples and enslave the inhabitants.

Athenian colonists cross to Oropus and march to join main Athenian force.

On the way to Marathon the Persians disembark the enslaved Eretrians on the island of Aigilia.

The Karystians attempt to resist the Persians but their lands are devastated until they submit.

Probable Athenian route to Marathon
Probable route of Athenian colonists
Probable Plataean route to Marathon
Persian fleet and army
Areas suitable for the landing and operation of the Persian cavalry

0   10 miles
0   20 km

According to Herodotus, when the fleet reached the bay of Marathon it was Hippias who had the ships anchor, disembarked the Persian forces and then arranged them in order of battle. The degree of influence Hippias had on Persian military activity is surely exaggerated. Herodotus' probable source is, after all, one of the Athenians accompanying Hippias. Nevertheless Datis was clearly relying heavily on his local knowledge. Many historians believe Datis landed at Marathon on the basis of Hippias' assurance that the region would rise in his support, as it had for his father half a century before. Herodotus makes no mention of this.

While Hippias was supervising the Persian disembarkation at Marathon he suffered a sudden coughing and sneezing fit. He was an old man, and so violent was his fit that he coughed out one of his teeth. But as hard as Hippias searched for it in the sand, he could not find it. In despair he took this as the fulfilment of his dream and cried out, 'This land is not ours, nor shall we subjugate it; for the share of it that was mine – the tooth has it.' The apparent interpretation of this dream and its consequences were perhaps clearer to Hippias than to the modern reader.

The Persian disembarkation, especially of the cavalry, must have taken a long time. The Persian ships anchored in the bay (Hdt. 6.107.2) rather than beached. Even if anchored several ships deep, the 600 vessels of the fleet must have stretched south-west for some considerable distance

Cape Kynosoura reaching out to sea like a twisting finger. The rocky knoll in the middle distance of this photograph reaches 92m above sea level, so the cape as a whole shelters Marathon Bay against the prevailing north-easterly winds.

along Schoinias beach. Such a large fleet certainly could not have all grouped together at the north-east end behind the shelter of Cape Kynosoura.

At the north-east end of the beach was a lake: the second key advantage of the site, since it enabled the Persians to water their horses. Six centuries later Pausanias (1.32.7) recorded a local legend that above the lake the stone mangers of Artaphernes' horses, and the marks of his tent could be seen on the rocks. It has been calculated that 1,000 horses require 8,000 gallons of water per day (Shrimpton 31 n. 23). Pausanias adds that a river flows out of this lake towards the sea. It is fresh enough to be drunk by cattle near the lake, but becomes salty and full of salt-water fish near its mouth. The Persians probably established their camp here on Schoinias Beach (Van Der Veer 298-9). Plutarch (*Mor.* 305B) says they camped and made war on the local population. Demosthenes (59. 94) also says they ravaged the area.

News of the landing reaches Athens

News of the Persian landing at Marathon probably reached Athens on the 8th day of *Metageitnion*, the second month of the Athenian lunar calendar. The date can be established by working back from the date of the arrival of Philippides, the Athenian herald, in Sparta. The Athenians probably sent him to Sparta immediately upon hearing of the landing. Herodotus (6.105) records that the Athenian generals were still in the city when the herald was sent.

An account of events in Athens is detailed by Nepos (*Milt.* 4.4). He says that first of all the Athenians created ten commanders, including Miltiades, to take charge of the army. This is a slight distortion. The *strategoi* would have taken up office at the beginning of the previous month, the start of the Athenian year. The *strategoi* debated whether to

Fragmentary bronze herald's wand (*kerykeion*) ending in Pan's head found on the Acropolis: perhaps referring to the vision of Philippides in 490. Hampe (*Die Antike* 15 (1939) 172) sought to link it to the figure atop the Kallimachos monument, which he identiified as Iris. It might simply be a fragment from a later herald's wand, Pan's head testifying to the help the god promised to the Athenian herald. (Athens, German Institute NM 4073, drawing Magdalena Wachnik)

wait behind their walls, or to go and meet the enemy and fight. Miltiades alone persistently urged the Athenians to take the field at the earliest possible moment. If they did so, Nepos records, 'not only would the citizens take heart when they saw that their courage was not disturbed, but for the same reason the enemy would be slower to act, if they realized that the Athenians dared to engage them with so small a force'. It is perhaps at this point that we should place the advice of Miltiades, as reported by Justin (2.9) that the army should not wait, thinking 'there was more trust to be placed in rapidity of action than in their allies'. Following this debate Miltiades moved a decree 'to set off once they have obtained food' to Marathon, which is mentioned by Demosthenes (19.303) and Aristotle (*Rhet.* 3.10.7).

It is not entirely clear whether the army marched out to Marathon immediately, or waited for Philippides to return. Justin (2.9) says they left when they found that the Lakedaimonians would be delayed four days as the result of a religious scruple. If Philippides reached Sparta on 9 Metageitnion, and returned to Athens on the 10th, reporting that the Lakedaimonians could only move on the 15th, then there would, indeed, remain four entire days when they could not move. So the Athenians may well have begun the march to Marathon on the 10 or 11 Metageitnion.

It was standard Greek practice to sacrifice a goat to Artemis Agroteria before any battle. Before Marathon a vow was made to sacrifice one goat a year for every enemy slain. Xenophon (*An.* 3.2.12) says it was 'the Athenians' who took the vow. After the battle they were unable to find as many goats as enemy they had slain, and instead offered 500. Does this mean that the whole Athenian citizen population took the oath? Surely not. An ancient commentator on Aristophanes' *Knights* 657 has Kallimachos make the vow to sacrifice as many oxen to Artemis Agroteria as barbarians killed. So many enemy were slain that, being unable to find so many oxen, they sacrificed goats instead. Kallimachos, as Polemarch, was responsible for the religious affairs of the army, so it is reasonable to assume that he took the oath on behalf of the Athenians. Aelian (*VH* 2.25) mistakenly attributes the vow to Miltiades and places the sacrifice on 6 Thargelion. In fact the festival of Artemis Agroteria took place on 6 Boedromion: the month following Metageitnion when the battle was fought. This may explain why Plutarch mistakenly fixes the date of the battle itself as 6 Boedromion in no less than three places (*Mor.* 349F, 861E; *Cam.* 19).

The herald's run to Sparta

The name of the herald sent to Sparta is generally rendered as Pheidippides (Badian), although it appears as Philippides in Herodotus and Plutarch (*Mor.* 862A). Philippides was an Athenian citizen and a 'day-runner' by profession. These 'day-runners' were couriers who could run the whole day delivering messages. Herodotus (6.106) says that Philippides arrived in Sparta the day after he had left Athens, the distance between the two cities being about 150 miles. Philippides came before the Lakedaimonian rulers and delivered the Athenian request for help. They replied that it was now the ninth day of the (second) lunar month, and they would have to wait until the full moon on the 15th before the army could march. In other Dorian states whose calendars are better preserved, such as Rhodes, the second lunar month of the year, beginning in late summer, is called *Karneios*: the month when the Karneian festival is held. So it seems that the Spartans did not have a ban on campaigning for the first half of every month, but only when the Karneia was being celebrated, during the waxing moon of the first half of the second month of the year.

Plato (*Laws* 3. 692D, 698E) gives other reasons for the delay. He says that the Lakedaimonains were one day late for the battle of Marathon because at that time they were engaged in war against the Messenians and had other difficulties. Plato's claim is supported by independent numismatic and epigraphic evidence (Wallace 32–5).

Philippides immediately ran back with the Spartan reply. He said he had met the god Pan while crossing Mount Parthenion above Tegea. Pan shouted his name 'Philippides' and asked him to relay the following words to the Athenians 'Why do you pay no attention to Pan, who is a good friend to the people of Athens, has helped you in the past, and will do so again?' In the sequence of events given by Herodotus it is implied that Philippides saw the god on his way to Sparta, but most modern scholars place the event on his return journey. The vision is best explained as a hallucination induced by exhaustion, and by Philippides' psychological need to find some compensation for the failure of his mission (Garland 50). The Athenians believed Philippides' story, says Herodotus (6.105), implying that he himself did not. According to Plutarch (*Mor.* 862B) the Athenian historian Diyllus records that on the proposal of Anytos the Athenians awarded Philippides ten talents for his feats on behalf of the city.

Mid-5th-century bronze statuette of Pan, 9cm high, from Lusoi in Arcadia. The god stands in the 'aposkopeuon' pose, shading his eyes from the sun as he gazes at a distant mountain. (Berlin, Staatliche Museen, Misc. 8624, photo Steinkopf)

PHILIPPIDES BEFORE THE SPARTAN EPHORS
(pages 38–39)

Herodotus tells us that Philippides made his appeal before the Spartan *archons*, or 'rulers', on the 9th day of the second lunar month. He presumably means the five *ephors* 'overlookers' – annually elected magistrates who had powers even over the two kings. When Philippides appealed to the *ephors* for Spartan aid against the Persians they replied that their army would not be able to march before the full moon on the 15th as they were celebrating a religious festival. The *ephors* did not reveal to Philippides the real reasons for their failure to send immediate aid to the Athenians; Sparta was in the midst of suppressing a Messenian revolt.

Philippides displays his badges of office, above all the bronze *kerykeion*, or herald's wand (1). These typically ended in two snake's heads, as shown here. Representations of Greek heralds, as opposed to Hermes, the messenger of the gods, are very rare. The other details of the figure are based on a representation of Agamemnon's herald Talthybios which appears on a *stamnos* (G 146) in the Louvre (*Warrior 27, Greek Hoplite*, N. Sekunda (Osprey 2000) 32). He wears a traveller's felt hat of the same shape as is normally worn by Hermes in art of the period (2). To a certain degree the hat too can be regarded as a symbol that the herald was under the protection of Hermes. It is shown in a medium brown

colour of natural felt: it may have been dyed a quite different colour. The highly elaborate boots (3) are also copied from the figure of Talthybios, but we do not know if they were regarded as typical for a herald, or were chosen at random by the vase-painter.

The ephors were members of the 'Spartiate' class who were noted for the uniformity of their dress, and their archaic hairstyles (4). They continued to wear long hair, a fashion long dead elsewhere among Greek aristocrats. The hair was braided into long locks all gathered together at the back, sometimes with a couple of locks allowed to fall loose. The thin Lakedaimonian cloak (*tribon*), tightly wrapped around the body, was worn in winter and summer alike to show the hardiness of the Spartan warriors to the cold (5). Ancient texts refer to the *tribon* being died crimson, a colour with military connotations among all ancient Greeks. Other texts mention single-soled red (not crimson) Lakonian shoes being worn by Lakonian sympathisers, such as Sophokles, in Athens. The shoes worn by the *ephors* (6) are based on a statue of Sophokles in the Vatican. The final 'badge' carried by all Spartiates was the 'crooked' walking stick (*bakterion*) they carried (7): smooth with a T-shaped crosspiece at the top, which enabled the carrier to rest by leaning on it.

The background shows the dispersed villages into which the ancient city of Sparta was divided, as viewed from the temple hill of the Amyklaion. (Richard Hook)

THE ATHENIAN MARCH TO MARATHON

According to Clement of Alexandria (*Stromata* 162,2) Miltiades led the Athenians to Marathon 'at night through places with no roads', but the second point at least is scarcely credible. There are two possible routes for an army to travel from Athens to Marathon. The main road passes through Pallene, skirts Mount Pentelikos to the south-east, and enters the plain of Marathon from the south-east. There is a second route, much less used, which travels north through Kephisia, skirts Pentelikos by the north-west and descends into the plain of Marathon from the west at Vrana. Though much rougher and steeper, it is slightly shorter. Berthold (1976/7) has detailed the reasons why the Athenians would have come by the longer route through Pallene. The Kephisia route, though shorter, would probably have taken much longer for such a large body of men (Burn 1977, 91). The Pallene route would also be taken by the Persian forces if they attempted to move inland against Athens, as it was the only one suitable for cavalry. The Athenians could not afford to let the Persians pass by them and reach Athens.

Herodotus (6.108) says the Athenian army camped in the sanctuary of Herakles (Herakleion) at Marathon. Here they were joined by the Plataeans, whose route is likewise uncertain. They may have crossed Mount Kithairon to Eleuthernai and then followed the internal Attic road system to Acharnai. From then on they too could have come by Pallene. Alternatively, they may have taken the road to Dekeleia, arriving in the Marathon plain from the west, or even from the north-west through Aphidna.

Debate of the Generals

The historical tradition reports a debate which took place between the Athenian generals once the army had reached Marathon. Herodotus (6.109) states that half of the *strategoi* did not want to give battle, as they believed the Athenian force was too small to achieve victory over the Persians. Suidas (*Hippias 2*) says they wanted to wait for the Lakedaimonians. The remaining five, led by Miltiades, were for fighting. Many historians believe that Herodotus has misplaced the debate, which logically ought to have taken place before the army marched out of the city. But if Herodotus is correct, something must have happened to cause the generals to have 'second thoughts'.

Diodorus (10.27) records that Datis made a final appeal for Athenian submission, placing it after the fall of Eretria. It is difficult to see when it might have been delivered other than on the eve of the battle. Datis appealed to the myth that the founder of the Median nation, Medos, had moved to Asia on being deprived of his lands by the Athenians. Medos was the oldest of his predecessors, and Datis said he had come to demand the return of the sovereignty belonging to his ancestors. If they surrendered, Datis promised to forgive the Athenians for this act, and for the sack of Sardis, but Athens would suffer the same fate as Eretria if they did not. It was perhaps during this exchange that Datis circulated the account of the 'netting' of Eretrian territory preserved by Plato. Raubitschek (1957) has suggested that 'the old song of Datis … How I am delighted and rejoiced and elated' at line 291 of the *Peace* of Aristophanes, parodies the preamble of this address of Datis to the Athenians.

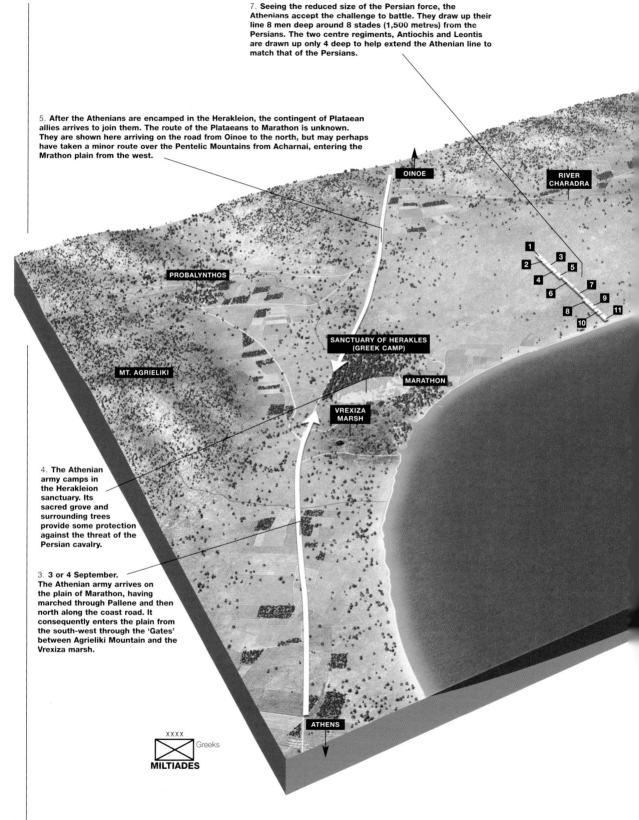

7. **Seeing the reduced size of the Persian force, the Athenians accept the challenge to battle. They draw up their line 8 men deep around 8 stades (1,500 metres) from the Persians. The two centre regiments, Antiochis and Leontis are drawn up only 4 deep to help extend the Athenian line to match that of the Persians.**

5. **After the Athenians are encamped in the Herakleion, the contingent of Plataean allies arrives to join them. The route of the Plataeans to Marathon is unknown. They are shown here arriving on the road from Oinoe to the north, but may perhaps have taken a minor route over the Pentelic Mountains from Acharnai, entering the Mrathon plain from the west.**

OINOE

RIVER CHARADRA

PROBALYNTHOS

1
2 3
4 5
6 7
8 9
10 11

SANCTUARY OF HERAKLES
(GREEK CAMP)

MT. AGRIELIKI

MARATHON

VREXIZA MARSH

4. **The Athenian army camps in the Herakleion sanctuary. Its sacred grove and surrounding trees provide some protection against the threat of the Persian cavalry.**

3. **3 or 4 September. The Athenian army arrives on the plain of Marathon, having marched through Pallene and then north along the coast road. It consequently enters the plain from the south-west through the 'Gates' between Agrieliki Mountain and the Vrexiza marsh.**

ATHENS

XXXX
Greeks
MILTIADES

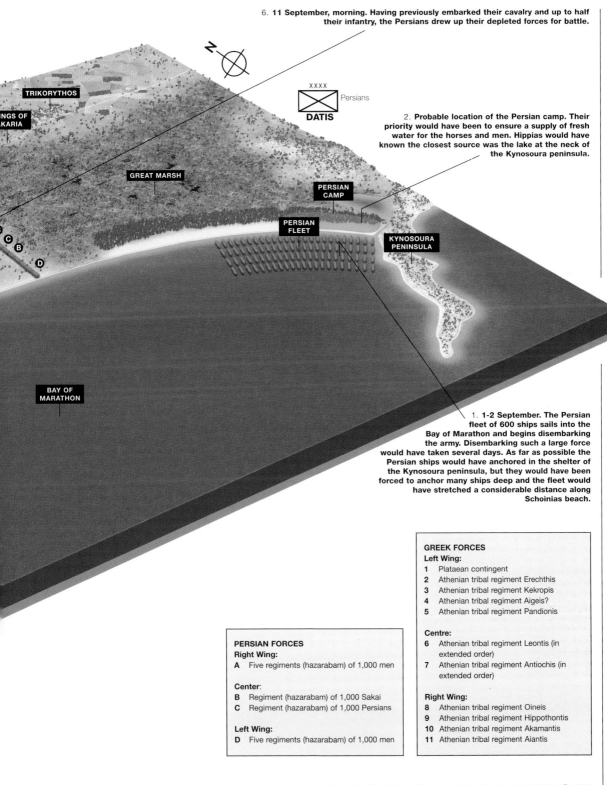

6. **11 September, morning.** Having previously embarked their cavalry and up to half their infantry, the Persians drew up their depleted forces for battle.

xxxx

DATIS Persians

2. **Probable location of the Persian camp.** Their priority would have been to ensure a supply of fresh water for the horses and men. Hippias would have known the closest source was the lake at the neck of the Kynosoura peninsula.

TRIKORYTHOS

RINGS OF AKARIA

GREAT MARSH

PERSIAN CAMP

PERSIAN FLEET

KYNOSOURA PENINSULA

C
B
D

BAY OF MARATHON

1. **1-2 September.** The Persian fleet of 600 ships sails into the Bay of Marathon and begins disembarking the army. Disembarking such a large force would have taken several days. As far as possible the Persian ships would have anchored in the shelter of the Kynosoura peninsula, but they would have been forced to anchor many ships deep and the fleet would have stretched a considerable distance along Schoinias beach.

GREEK FORCES
Left Wing:
1 Plataean contingent
2 Athenian tribal regiment Erechthis
3 Athenian tribal regiment Kekropis
4 Athenian tribal regiment Aigeis?
5 Athenian tribal regiment Pandionis

Centre:
6 Athenian tribal regiment Leontis (in extended order)
7 Athenian tribal regiment Antiochis (in extended order)

Right Wing:
8 Athenian tribal regiment Oineis
9 Athenian tribal regiment Hippothontis
10 Athenian tribal regiment Akamantis
11 Athenian tribal regiment Aiantis

PERSIAN FORCES
Right Wing:
A Five regiments (hazarabam) of 1,000 men

Center:
B Regiment (hazarabam) of 1,000 Sakai
C Regiment (hazarabam) of 1,000 Persians

Left Wing:
D Five regiments (hazarabam) of 1,000 men

BATTLE OF MARATHON

1-11 September 490BC, viewed from the south-west, showing the deployment of the Persian and Greek forces in the plain of Marathon

Another cup by the same painter as the Oxford Brygos was once on the art market in Rome, but is now lost and only preserved in drawings. Painted shortly after Marathon, it probably shows the men of an Athenian family, veterans of the battle as is made clear by the shield-devices of Marathonian bulls, preparing to march against the enemy. On side A (top) a female, perhaps the warrior's wife, pours wine for the seated figure of Zeus, who watches the grandfather, beard and hair shorn in mourning, say goodbye to his son. On side B (bottom right) the grandfather watches his two eldest grandsons arm, on the right his daughter-in-law hands her husband his sword. The tondo (below) is probably meant to represent the grandfather together with the youngest grandson – both either too young or too old to go and fight. (Rome, Istituto Archeologico Germanico neg 75. 1682–4)

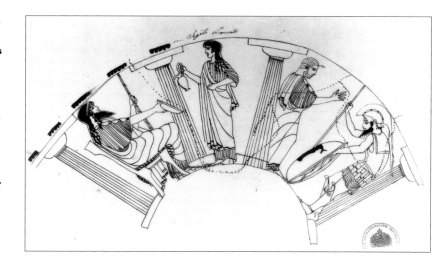

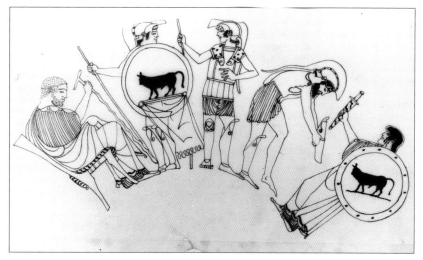

If this appeal for submission is truly historical, it implies that Datis' original orders were not to enslave the Eretrians and Athenians under all circumstances, but only if he could not ensure their submission.

The group of generals opposed to battle may have been led by Aristeides. A few years later he was ostracized from Athens. Some of the *ostraka* cast against him describe him as 'the traitor'. As Polemarch, Kallimachos of Aphidna had the deciding vote. Herodotus has Miltiades address him with the following stirring words:

> *It lies in your hands, Kallimachos, whether to enslave Athens or keep her free and thereby leave a memorial for all the life of mankind, such as not even Harmodios and Aristogeiton left behind them. For the Athenians were never in so great danger from the time they were first a people. And if they succumb to the Medes, it has been determined what they are to suffer, when delivered up to Hippias; but if the city survives, it will become first among all the Greek cities. How, then, all this can happen, and why it depends on you to decide I shall explain.*
>
> *The opinions of us strategoi, who are ten, are divided: the one party urging that we should engage; the other that we should not engage. Now*

if we do not engage, I expect that some great dissension arising among us will shake the minds of the Athenians and persuade them to Medize. But if we fight before this rottenness starts to infect some of the Athenians, we may well win the fight if the gods treat us fairly. All these things, therefore, are now in your power and entirely depend on you. For if you will support my opinion, your country will be free, and the city the first in Greece; but if you join with those who would turn away from the fight, the exact opposite of the good things I have described will fall to you.

These are unlikely to be Miltiades' actual words. He hardly needed to remind Kallimachos that there were ten *strategoi* – this is included for the readership. Kallimachos, of course, decided in favour of giving battle. According to Diodorus (10.27) Miltiades, 'voicing the decision reached by the ten generals' personally delivered the reply to the Persian envoys. He replied that according to the myth cited by Datis, it was more appropriate for the Athenians to hold mastery over Media than Datis over Athens, for it was a man of Athens who had established the kingdom of the Medes, whereas no man of Median race had ever controlled Athens.

The church of Agios Demetrios viewed from the road to Marathon Museum at Vrana. Sotiriadis, who carried out extensive field work in the plain between 1926 and 1940, thought he had found traces of the Herakleion here. In the background the slopes of the Agrilieki mountain.

THE BATTLEFIELD

Any account of the battle must be based on a sound reconstruction of the appearance of the battlefield in September 490BC. Our improving knowledge of the ancient landscape has meant that many earlier reconstructions are no longer tenable. In what follows I have tried to summarize current topographical knowledge. The maps in this book are a personal interpretation.

Petrakos (2) writes that the plain derives its name from the wild fennel (*marathos*) that grows all over it to this day. This is about the only constant feature of the plain over two and a half millennia. We cannot even be certain where the ancient village of Marathon lay. The Marathon plain has changed vastly over the past two centuries. The huge growth of Athens has turned the Marathon plain into a fruit and vegetable garden. It is lush with vegetable crops planted between lines of trees, irrigated with groundwater, and tended by South Asian labourers. Photographs from the early 20th century show the plain only lightly planted with olives and other trees, and with few if any crops between the rows of trees.

We have a good idea of how the plain looked at the start of the 19th century, thanks to Colonel Leake, a British agent gathering topographical information during the Napoleonic wars. Colonel Leake, who visited the Marathon plain on a number of occasions beginning in 1802, described it in the following terms (Grote 273 n. 1): 'It is moderately cultivated with corn, and is one of the most fertile spots in Attica, though rather inconveniently subject to inundations from the two torrents which cross it … the circumstances of the battle incline one to believe that it was

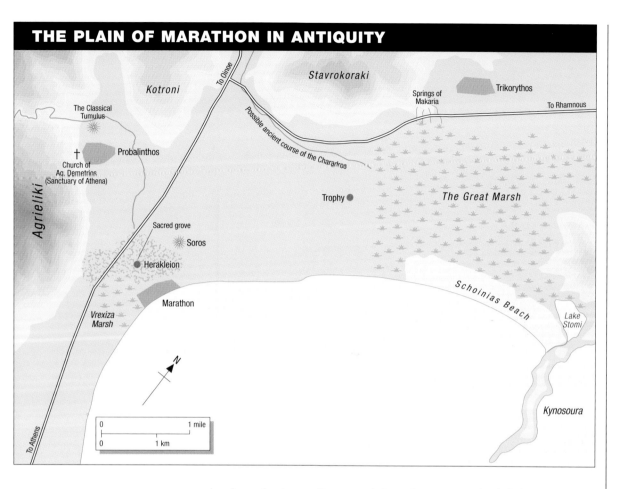

anciently as destitute of trees as it is at the present day.' Colonel Leake is doubtless correct. In antiquity the plain would be partly planted with cereals, but for the most part left fallow for grazing. Aristophanes (*Birds* 245–6) refers to the beautiful meadows of Marathon. Edward Dodwell, who visited Marathon at the beginning of the 19th century, also remarked on the number of cattle grazing on the uncultivated areas of the plain in late June. Indeed, the symbol of Marathon was the Marathonian bull, which had terrified the 'Tetrapolis' (the four settlements of the Marathon plain) until mastered by the Athenian hero Theseus and sacrificed to Apollo (Plut., *Thes.* 14.1).

The location of the Herakleion is the key to understanding the battlefield. Professor George Soteriades thought the Herakleion might be located near the church of Agios Giorgios at Vrana. In 1933 he reported the discovery of an inscribed boundary stone from a sanctuary of Athena in this area, along with a dedicatory inscription by one Theogenes of Probalinthos (Vanderpool 1966). These finds locate the site of the ancient village of Probalinthos here, together with a sanctuary of Athena, probably Athena Hellotis (Hammond 1968, 24).

The later discovery of two inscriptions in the area of Valaria mentioning the cult of Herakles enabled Vanderpool (1966) to locate the Herakleion there: possibly near the site of the church of the Saints Theodore. In one inscription the god is called Herakles *Empylian* 'at the gates'. The gap between Agrieliki and the Vrexiza marsh leading out of the Marathon plain

At the south-west entrance to the Marathon plain the Agrilieki mountain stretches down towards the coast leaving (as here) only a narrow stretch of land between it and (to our backs in this photograph) the Vrexiza marsh and then the sea. This was the site of the shrine of Herakles 'at the Gates' and of the Athenian camp.

towards Athens seems to have seen called *Pylai* or 'Gates' in antiquity. The second deals with the founding of the Herakleian Games after the battle (Petrakos 50–2, 137–40). Pindar's *Eighth Pythian Ode*, perhaps composed in 446, mentions the victory of Aristomenes of Aegina in the Herakleian Games, and (line 79) locates his victory in the 'innermost nook' of Marathon. 'This may be a support for Vanderpool's view: the oblong southern entrance into which the narrowing plain leads can be conceived as a recess or nook' (Van Der Veer 297).

This confined space offered the Greeks an ideal defensive position, although by late summer the Vrexiza marsh would probably have been almost dry (Grote 273). The Athenian army would still have been able to draw water from a number of springs rising at the foot of the Agrieliki mountain which once fed the marsh, and which are shown on early maps.

The sanctuary lay inside a sacred grove. The funeral epitaph of Aischylos (Athenaeus 14.627D; Paus. 1.14.5) mentions that the fighting took place in the Marathonian *alsos*, or 'sacred grove', evidently of olives for Nonnus (13.189) refers to the sacred precinct at olive-growing Marathon thick with trees. In Seneca's *Hippolytus* 17–8 King Hippolytus of Athens orders his huntsmen to take the left path which comes out of the wood at Marathon. The description of both the *alsos* and the Herakleion as being 'Marathonian' suggest that the village of Marathon lay nearby. It therefore appears on our maps between the Heraklion, the Vrexiza marsh, and the coast, in roughly the same location as the modern settlement of Marathon Beach.

Both the Vrexiza marsh and the Great Marsh were drained in the late 1920s and early 1930s as part of the Rockerfeller Foundation's international campaign against malaria. The area covered by both marshes in our reconstructions is based on their extent before drainage. There are ancient references to marshy ground at Marathon, such as Aristotle, *History of Animals* 6.15. An ancient commentator on Plato, *Menexenus* 240 C describes the plain as 'rocky by nature, difficult for horses, with mud, swamps and lakes inside it'. The Makaria springs

OPPOSITE
After the road to Kato-Souli and Rhamnous forks off the main road from Athens to the modern town of Marathon, it crosses the bed of the Charadra. Here WW2 anti-tank ditches, mentioned by Pritchett (1960, 157) show quite clearly the strata of river boulders washed into the plain by flash floods.

rising from the foot of Stavrokoraki fed the Great Marsh. This was the site of the ancient village of Trikorythos. Aristophanes (*Lysistrata* 1032) uses the term 'Trykorysian mosquito', which the commentary on the passage explains as follows: 'Tricorysian mosquito because there are a lot of mosquitos at Trikorythos. This place is rich in greenery and very wet.'

Marathon was described as a Tetrapolis, or 'Quadruple City', in antiquity. The fourth town was Oinoe, just outside the plain to the north-west, close to the modern town of Marathon. A torrent, known as the Charadra in ancient and modern times alike, ran into the plain from Oinoe, between Tsepi and Stavrokoraki and regularly flooded it. 'The Oinoe Torrent' became proverbial, and a fragment of Demon contained in Hesychius (Hammond 1968, 53) refers to its flooding. Colonel Leake noted that the torrent is 'still noted for the quantity of water which is sometimes brought down by it, and for the mischief caused by its occasional impetuosity. In the autumn of 1805, the torrent carried away some of the houses of the village of Seferi, and destroyed cattle and corn-fields in the great plain below. Soon afterwards I found the appearance of this village quite altered from that which it had presented me on two earlier visits to Marathon'.

Early maps of the Marathon plain, particularly that of Fauvel, show the Charadra draining into the bay of Marathon much further towards the north-east than in modern times. Evidently the course of the river often shifts during its periodic flash floods. Pritchett (1960, 157), after consultation with Professor C. Higgins of the University of California at Davis, suggested that the Charadra probably ran into the Great Marsh in antiquity. It is shown as such in the artwork. This would have meant that a greater quantity of fresh water ran into the Great Marsh. In modern

ABOVE
Head of the river god Archeloos, lord of the violent force of the Charadra, found near Marathon and acquired for Berlin Museum in 1848 through the help of Schaubert, the German architect and town-planner responsible for designing Athens as Greece's capital for the new King Otto of Bavaria. The Pentelic marble head dates to about 470 and comes from a shrine somewhere on the plain of Marathon. (Berlin, Staatliche Museen)

times the fresh water flowing through the Great Marsh from Makaria gathered into Lake Stomi, a fresh-water lake lying between Drakonera and Kynosoura. Pausanias (1.32.7) confirms that this lake existed in antiquity.

The question of where the ancient shoreline ran in Marathon Bay has recently been politicised by the construction of facilities for the Olympic Games in what little remains of the unexploited areas of the Great Marsh. Excavation of the Sorós confirmed that about 3m of alluvial material have been deposited on the surface of the plain as it existed in the 5th century BC (Pritchett 1960, 141). This is only to be expected given the violent activity of the Charadra. The area is still tectonically active, however, and there is strong evidence that the coastline has been oscillating by only relatively small distances (Pritchett 1965, 83-4). It would be reasonable to assume that the shore in the 5th century BC was in roughly the same position as it is now.

PRELUDE TO BATTLE

The battle probably took place on seventeenth day of the Athenian month Metageitnion, which in 490BC corresponds to 11 September (Hammond 1968, 40 n.121). This date is arrived at by calculating forward from Herodotus (6.106.3), who states that Philippides reached Sparta on 9 Metageitnion. The Spartans could not move before the full moon, which would have been on the 15th. They reached Athens on the third day after leaving Sparta (Hdt. 6.120) – the 18th – arriving one day too late for the battle, as Plato (*Laws* 698E) states. Thus the battle took place on the 17th of the month. The Athenian army must have marched to Marathon on the 11th at the latest, even assuming they had waited for

Philippides to return with the Lakedaimonian reply. So the two rival armies must have faced each other for at least five or six days without engaging.

It is reasonable to assume that the Greeks delayed action while awaiting the arrival of the Spartans, but it is less easy to understand why Datis did not attack. The confusing text of Nepos *Militiades* 5 has been interpreted in several ways. I follow the translation of J.C. Rolfe. Nepos says that the Athenians set out from Athens and camped in a favourable position:

'Then on the following day, the army was drawn up at the foot of the mountain in a part of the plain that was not wholly open – for there were isolated trees in many places – and they joined battle. The purpose was to protect themselves by the high mountains, and at the same time prevent the enemy's cavalry, hampered by the scattered trees, from surrounding them with their superior numbers.'

Presumably Nepos means that they drew up their line within the sacred grove, in front of the Herakleion, running from the protection afforded by the Agrilieki mountain on their left flank, down to the sea upon which their right flank rested. This would explain why Datis was unable to attack them, as he was unable to bring his cavalry into action. Datis knew his cavalry was his battle-winning asset. Presumably he was unwilling to risk a purely infantry engagement.

Some historians have interpreted the Nepos passage to mean that the Athenians themselves scattered the 'trees' in many places: that is they constructed an *abatis*. There is some support for this interpretation. If Frontinus (*Strat.* 2.2.9) is to be believed, in 510, when the Spartan king Kleomenes invaded Attica to liberate it from the Tyrant Hippias, he also employed an *abatis* against the Thessalian cavalry fighting for Hippias. It seems preferable, however, to take Nepos' words at face value.

Datis divides his forces

Under these circumstances the onus to break the deadlock was on Datis. He must have known, through intelligence gathered from the adherents of Hippias, that the Spartans would move after the full moon. Indeed Nepos (*Milt.* 5. 4) states that Datis wished to give battle before the Lakedaimonians arrived. Once they arrived, he would continue to have an outright advantage in his cavalry, but would lose much of the numerical superiority he enjoyed in infantry. Under the pressure of these considerations, it seems that Datis decided to split his forces. A Greek saying mentioned in the *Lexicon* of Suidas may give us a clue on why he did this:

'*Choris Hippeis* (The cavalry are away) – Datis having invaded Attica, they say that the Ionians on his going back went up to the trees and made signs to the Athenians that the cavalry were away; and Miltiades on becoming aware of their withdrawal engaged on those terms and was victorious. That is why the proverb is used of those who break formation'.

The Ionians may well have gone 'up to the trees', that is inland to the sacred grove the night before the battle to tell the Athenians that Datis had decided to split his forces and embark the cavalry (Hammond 1968,

One of Artaphernes' cavalrymen may be shown on this cup in the Faina Collection (no. 48) in Orvieto, where it was found. The letters *omicron* and *rho* of an inscription can just be made out painted above the left upper arm of the rider. According to Williams (75–6) the letters are short for *Choris Hippeis* 'the cavalry are away', and the vase was painted by Antiphon in the year of the battle of Marathon or shortly after. (Rome, Istituto Archeologico Germanico neg. 61.1192)

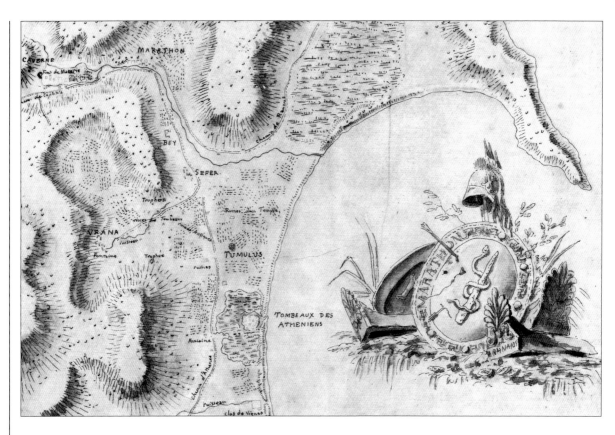

The earliest modern map of the Marathon plain is the 1792 map of L.F.S. Fauvel, the French consul to Greece. It shows the main course of the Charadra stream running much further to the east, behind the 'Ruines d'une Temple' in the centre of the map, which presumably marks the ruins of the Frankish Tower near the church of Panaghia Mesosporitisa. (Paris, Bibliothéque Nationale, Collection Barbier no. 1341)

39–40). Presumably the horses had been loaded aboard their transports in daytime. Embarking horses by day was a difficult enough task (Evans 1987, 104) without adding the difficulties of attempting it in darkness.

The split of forces may also perhaps be implied in Nepos' statement that Datis led out 100,000 infantry to battle (as well as 10,000 horse it should be added), after writing earlier that the infantry accompanying the expedition totalled 200,000 (How & Welles 361). Nepos' source evidently believed that Datis fought Marathon with only half the troops he had available.

It must be stressed that Herodotus makes no mention of any split in forces. Suidas is a very late source, and many are unwilling to believe such an important event could have been overlooked by Herodotus and other earlier sources. But then it is hardly more probable that an early medieval writer made up both an ancient proverb and its explanation.

The aim of Datis in splitting his forces must surely have been to use half to pin down the Athenian army, while the other half, together with the cavalry, made an attempt on Athens while her army was away, and before the Spartans arrived. Presumably the intention was to land in the bay of Phaleron, which the Persians in the end attempted following their defeat. I assume that the Persians had broken camp and taken all tents aboard the ships, as there is no mention of the capture of the Persian camp in Herodotus. When it became clear that the Greeks would offer battle, the Persian fleet remained anchored in the bay. It is unlikely that any of the Persian commanders expected defeat.

Operational command of the Athenian forces rotated on a daily basis among the ten *strategoi*. According to Herodotus (6.110) whenever it was

The olive trees of the sacred grove at Marathon hampered the movement of the Persian cavalry. We get some idea of what the sacred grove would have looked like from these olives growing about the base of the Sorós monument.

the turn of one of the five *strategoi* who had sided with Miltiades to command the army, they had handed over command to him. Miltiades, however, delayed taking action until the day of his own command came round. However Plutarch (*Arist.* 5.2) has Aristeides, in command of the tribal regiment of Antiochis, hand over his command to Miltiades on the day of the battle. It is interesting to note that the days of command of Oineis, Miltiades' tribe, and Antiochis, Aristeides' tribe came next to one another in the order of precedence established by Raubitschek (see Athenian order of battle, p.54). It may be that command was moving one tribe to the left each day, starting with Aiantis on the right flank, from the day when the Athenian army was first drawn up for battle at Marathon. If this supposition is correct, Oineis would have held command on the fourth day of the stand-off and Antiochis on the fifth.

THE BATTLE

It seems that the Persians drew up for battle first. Herodotus (6.113) specifically mentions that 'the Persians themselves' and the Sakai were stationed in the centre of the Persian line. This is as we would expect, for it was Persian practice to command the line from the centre, and Datis would have stationed himself there. The 'Persians' would have been the regiment of 1,000 *arstibara* escorting Datis. The Sakai would comprise the other two or three elite infantry *hazarabam* of the centre. If my speculation is correct half a *baivarabam* would be drawn up on either side of the centre. It was standard Persian practice to draw up infantry formations ten deep, so the frontage of the line would have been about 1,400 men. The Aeolian and Ionian contingents accompanying the army are not mentioned in any account of the battle. Presumably they were already embarked on the ships.

THE ATHENIAN ORDER OF BATTLE

	Late Fifth/Early Fourth Centuries	Order in Pollux as chosen by Apollo	Reconstruction of Raubitschek (1956)
			[Aigeis (II) uncertain]
1	Erechtheis (I)	Erechtheis (I)	Erechtheis (I)
2	Aigeis (II)	Kekropis (VII)	Kekropis (VII)
3	Pandionis (III)	[Aigeis (II)]	
4	Leontis (IV)	Pandionis (III)	Pandionis (III)
5	Akamantis (V)	[Akamantis (V)]	Leontis (IV)
6	Oineis (VI)	Antiochis (X)	Antiochis (X)
7	Kekropis (VII)	Leontis (IV)	Oineis (VI)
8	Hippothontis (VIII)	Oineis (VI)	Hippothontis (VIII)
9	Aiantis (IX)	Hippothontis (VIII)	Akamantis (V)
10	Antiochis (X)	Aiantis (IX)	Aiantis (IX)

The Athenians now drew up their line of battle. Herodotus (6.111) mentions that their line was equal in length to the Persian formation, the middle of the line being only a few ranks deep, the army being weakest at this point, but each of the two wings was strong in number. The normal depth of the Greek phalanx was 8 deep. Although this is pure speculation, 'a few ranks' might mean that the tribes in the centre were drawn up 4 deep, while the tribes on the two flanks were left 8 deep (Lazenby 64). If the Plataeans and eight of the Athenian tribes were drawn up 8 deep, and the two Athenian tribes holding the centre were reduced to 4 deep, then the frontage would be about the same as the Persian (1,475 men). The speculative nature of this calculation must be emphasized.

Herm of Aischylos in Naples Archaeological Museum (6139). Born in 525, he fought at Marathon, Artemision, Salamis and then Plataea. According to the *Marmor Parium* ep. 48 he fought at Marathon with some distinction. The battle evidently made a great impression on him. In later life he lost his hair, and according to one legend he died in Gela aged 69, when an eagle smashed a turtle against his head, mistaking it for a rock. His funeral epitaph states that 'the grove of Marathon can vouch for his famed valour, and the long-haired Mede who knew it well'. (Rome, Istituto Archeologico Germanico)

A number of sources confirm that the tribal regiment Aiantis (IX) fought on the right flank. Plutarch (*Mor.* 628E) says that 'The orator Glaukias said that the right flank of the battle-line at Marathon was given to the men of Aiantis; this he based on the elegaic poem of Aischylos 'who fought brilliantly in that battle'. Aischylos son of Euphorion was of the deme Eleusis of the tribe Aiantis, and fought in this tribal regiment alongside his brother Kynegeiros, who died in the fighting over the Persian ships. Elsewhere in his *Moralia* (305B) Plutarch makes Kynegeiros *strategos* of the tribe Aiantis, but this is almost certainly incorrect. Justin (2.9) specifically calls Kynegeiros a common soldier (*miles*). In the same passage Plutarch makes all sorts of unlikely individuals *strategoi*, Kallimachos the Polemarch becomes one, as does Polyzelos – a mistake for the common soldier Epizelos son of Kouphagos who was struck blind during the battle. The *strategos* of the regiment was probably Stesileos who is later mentioned as falling in the battle at the ships, in which Aiantis was most heavily, and perhaps solely, engaged. Three of the demes of the Marathonian Tetrapolis, Marathon, Oinoe and Trikorynthos, formed one of the trittyes of Aiantis. The men of Probalinthos fought in Pandionis.

Herodotus (6.111) notes that Kallimachos led the right wing of the line, 'for the law at that time among the Athenians demanded that the Polemarch should have the right wing'. By coincidence this placed Kallimachos with his own tribal regiment, since his deme, Aphidna, belonged to Aiantis.

Plutarch (*Arist.* 5.3) mentions that Themistokles son of Neokles of the deme Phrearrhioi and Aristeides son of Lysimachos of the deme Alopeke fought side by side in the battle, for they fought in the tribes Leontis (IV) and Antiochis (X) respectively. These two tribes fought in the centre of the Greek line. Plutarch (5.1) specifically mentions that Aristides held the office of *strategos* of Antiochis, and a number of

Present-day remains of the Frankish Tower in the grounds of the church of Panaghia Mesosporitisa. The tower incorporated elements from a marble column, capital, and crowning figure, as well as other ancient construction blocks probably from a tomb dating to the third quarter of the 4th century BC. The construction was taken apart, the marble elements were removed, and the remaining blocks were put back together again.

modern historians have inferred from this that Plutarch implies that Themistokles was correspondingly *strategos* of Leontis. This does not necessarily follow, although Justin (2.9) mentions that Themistokles, though only a young man, distinguished himself in the battle for his heroism, giving the first indication of his future greatness as a military leader. In fact Themistokles was born about 528, so would have been 38 when the battle was fought. He had already held the office of *archon* in 493, so there is no reason why he may not have served as *strategos* for Leontis in 490. Miltiades would have been *strategos* of the tribe Oineis (VI) but no source states where this tribe stood in the line.

Herodotus says the Athenian tribes were drawn up 'alongside one another according to their number'. Most historians think this means in their official order of precedence, Pritchett (1960, 147) thinks it may mean by strength. The two may be the same if precedence was based on the relative strength of the tribes. The known positions of the three tribes mentioned above in the line at Marathon is at variance with the standard order of precedence which became established in the later 5th century and continued to be used throughout the 4th. Two other lists of tribal precedence are also available (see Athenian order of battle. p.54). The first is the order of the ten tribal names selected from the list of 100 submitted to the oracle of Apollo at Delphi in 508/07, preserved in Pollux *Onomasticon* (8.110). Two tribes, Aigeis and Akamantis [listed in square brackets] are missing in some manuscripts and may have been added in the others, and so their position is not certain. Raubitschek (1956) would alter the order in Pollux slightly to bring it into line with early 5th-century inscriptions demarcating the order in which the tribes had to stand in the Peiraieus when the fleet was manned, or in the Agora

when voting. He would take out Aigeis, whose place is uncertain, place Akamantis between Hippothontis and Aiantis, and reverse the order of Antiochis and Leontis. He notes, however, a number of other early 5th-century tribal lists which are 'out of order', before the later canonical order becomes standard. As can be seen, the order of tribes given by Pollux or built up by Raubitschek would fit what we know of the Athenian line at Marathon. Raubitschek's order is perhaps preferable, as it places Antiochis and Leontis closer to the centre of the line.

The Plataean contingent, as was normal for allies fighting outside their native country, fought on the left flank.

Location of the battle

Modern historians have positioned the Athenian and Persian lines on the plain of Marathon in a variety of ways, mainly depending on whether they have located the Herakleion and the Athenian camp at Agios Demetrios or at Valaria. Many early reconstructions had the Persians fighting parallel to the coast with their backs to the sea. This helped explain how they fled to their ships, and how they pushed the Athenian centre 'inland', but failed to explain how and why their wings fled into the Great Marsh. This is the reconstruction followed in recent times by Hammond.

This map of the Marathon Plain published by H.G. Lolling records (in red) the location of many ancient monuments still surviving in his day, but now lost. One of these is the Pyrgos, which some would identify as the site of the Miltiades monument. (After *Athenische Mitteilungen* 1 (1876) pl. iv)

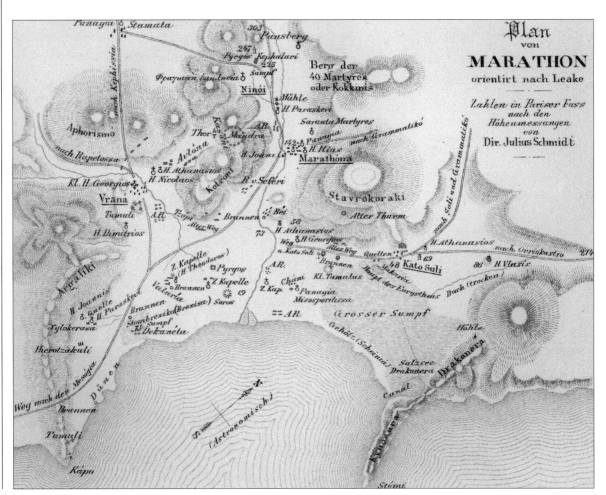

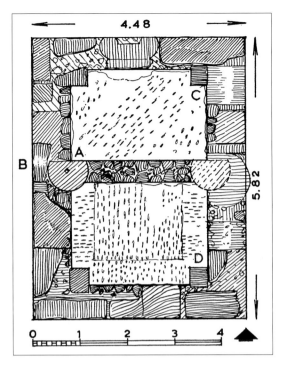

4.48

5.82

0 1 2 3 4

Drawing of the Ionic capital which once crowned the Trophy monument and plan of the Frankish Tower before excavation, by John Travlos (*Hesperia* 35 (1966) 95, 98). In the plan the capital is shown at top, and the four column-drums are marked by the letters A–D. The column drums and capital of this monument have been partially reconstructed and are on display in Marathon Museum. The reconstruction drawing of the monument as a whole is by I. Yarmenitis. (Athens Archaeological Sociey)

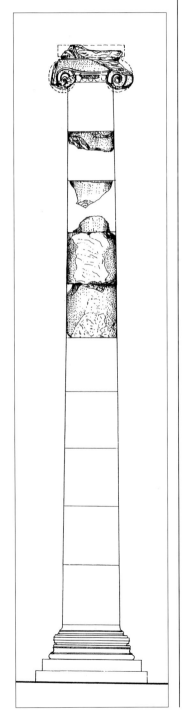

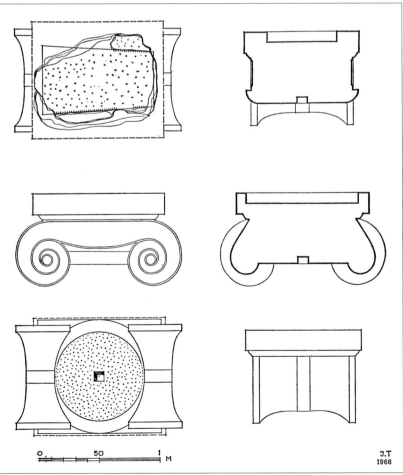

0 50 1 M

J.T
1966

Arrow and spear heads gathered from the excavation of a 'grave in the plain', presumably the Sorós, carried out in 1830 by Admiral Brock, later deposited in the British Museum. The arrowheads compare well with known western Iranian types. (Trustees British Museum)

It seems that General Sir Frederick Maurice was the first to suggest that the opposing lines were drawn up perpendicular to the coast rather than parallel. He believed that the Persians would have drawn their line up on the Charadra, taking advantage of its steep banks, which are as much as 18ft high in places (Pritchett 1960, 156). I follow Pritchett in the belief that the Charadra flowed into the Great Marsh in antiquity, so I do not think that this could have been a consideration. Even if the Charadra did flow over the field of battle in 490, it is not mentioned in any sources describing the fighting, suggesting it played no significant role in the battle (Van Der Veer 305–6). Like Pritchett, I accept Maurice's configuration for the opposing battlelines, even if I do not accept his reasoning.

To stand any chance of being close to the realities of the battle fought some 2,500 years ago, our reconstruction must take into account the likely starting-point of both lines, the probable length of both battlelines, and any further clues supplied by the ancient topography. We know that the Athenian camp was at the Herakleion near Valaria, and it is highly probable that the Persian camp was somewhere in the area of Schoinias beach. It seems an almost inevitable conclusion that the two lines were drawn up at right angles to the coast. This disposition alone would explain why the majority of the Persian line fled into the Great Marsh. As has already been explained, both lines would have been about 1,500 men, paces, yards or metres long, and, as will be explained shortly, the Athenians started their advance from a position about 1,500m from the Persians.

The ancient topography also supplies us with some clues. Increasingly intensive agricultural exploitation over the past two centuries has largely obliterated the traces of ancient constructions which were once numerous in the plain. Archaeologists such as Soteriades and Vanderpool have rescued much information, and some further details can be recovered from old maps, such as that of Lolling. Pausanias (1.32.3–5) mentions that when he visited the central part of the Marathon plain, he saw the tomb of the Athenians, the tomb of the Plataeans and slaves, a monument to Miltiades, and a trophy of white marble. It is generally assumed that all these monuments lay close together, and that Pausanias visited them in turn (Hammond 1968, 18).

The Sorós must be identified as the tomb of the Athenians. The early travellers Clarke and Leake both reported seeing a smaller tumulus near the Sorós, which they thought might be the tomb of the Plataeans and slaves. The Pyrgos, marked about 600–700m north of the Sorós on old maps, was a medieval tower apparently built of ancient materials, which has now disappeared. It may have been constructed from materials taken from the Miltiades monument (Vanderpool 1966, 101), or from the Sanctuary of Dionysos – the religious centre of the Marathon Tetrapolis (Van Der Veer 292–3).

The surviving foundation course of a second medieval tower has been shown to incorporate elements from 'the trophy of white marble'. This tower is located in the grounds of the Church of Panaghia Mesosporitisa. This identification was first proposed by Colonel Leake in 1829 but only confirmed by the excavation of Eugene Vanderpool in 1965. Vanderpool interpreted the marble column as a Kimonian construction dating to around 460 to glorify the memory of his father. It would have replaced an earlier, much simpler, trophy erected there immediately after the battle.

Of all these four monuments it is the trophy which is the most valuable for our reconstruction of the topography of the battle. The Greeks normally erected a victory trophy at the point where the 'turn-round' (*trope*) of the enemy had first occurred. The original trophy is not likely to have stood at any great distance from the site of the tower when it was demolished for building materials. The church of Panaghia Mesosporitisa lies about 1,500 paces from the sea. The Persian line did not advance during the battle, except for the centre, which managed to push back the Athenian centre after it had received the charge of the latter. Therefore it seems plausible to draw up the Persian line at the beginning of the battle with its left flank resting on the shore, and its right flank positioned around the area of Panaghia Mesosporitisa, or perhaps a little forward of it, and its back to the Great Marsh. The Greek line would therefore be drawn up parallel some 1,500m to the south-west with its right flank resting on the sea.

Following the battle the tribal regiment Antiochis was left behind to guard the prisoners and to collect the dead. During the battle Antiochis and Leontis had both been pushed back by the Persians and Sakai in the centre. Although some Athenian casualties would have been caused by Persian archery during the charge, it is reasonable to assume that the majority had been killed when the two regiments in the centre were pushed back. In hand-to-hand fighting in general, and in hoplite warfare in particular, whenever an infantry force turned its back on its victorious enemy, it rendered itself practically defenceless. The actual earth tumulus of the Sorós seems to be another Kimonian construction, but equally almost certainly on the site of the original mass burial after the battle. The Sorós lies more than 3km south-west of the church of Panaghia Mesosporitisa, but about 750m from the sea, and so it must lie some distance behind the centre of the Athenian start-line, indeed about half-way back towards the Athenian camp at the Herakleion. Perhaps its location is best explained as the place where Antiochis and Leontis rallied themselves after being pushed back. It was perhaps at this spot that they first began the difficult and unpleasant task of gathering the bodies of the dead, and this is why the dead were later buried at that spot.

One possible objection is that a number of arrowheads, certainly Persian and associated with the battle, have been found in the fill over the Sorós. It could be argued that they indicate that the Sorós lay within the field of Persian archery during the battle. Therefore the main battle should have taken place here, further to the south-west than in my construction. However, the nearer the site of the main battle moves towards the Sorós, the further it moves away from the site of the remains of the trophy. It is probable that the soil needed to erect the Sorós would

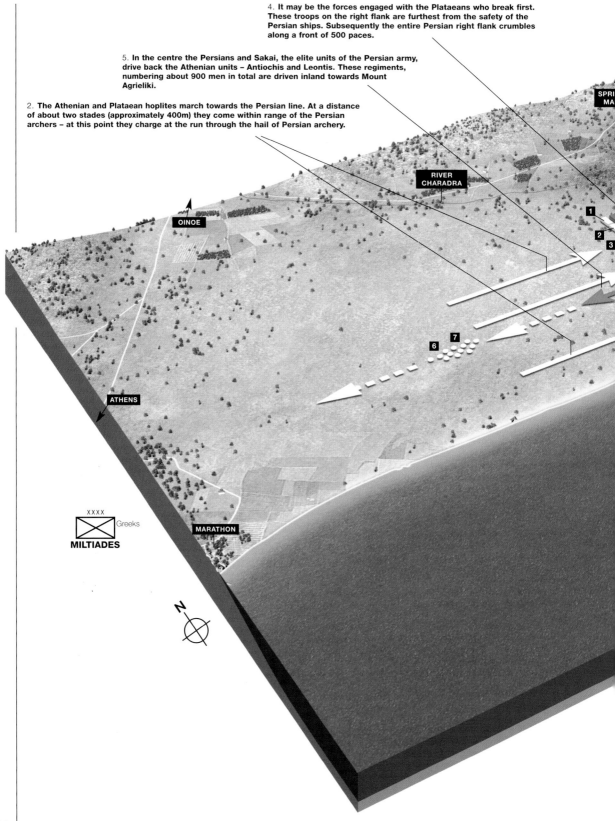

4. **It may be the forces engaged with the Plataeans who break first. These troops on the right flank are furthest from the safety of the Persian ships. Subsequently the entire Persian right flank crumbles along a front of 500 paces.**

5. **In the centre the Persians and Sakai, the elite units of the Persian army, drive back the Athenian units – Antiochis and Leontis. These regiments, numbering about 900 men in total are driven inland towards Mount Agrieliki.**

2. **The Athenian and Plataean hoplites march towards the Persian line. At a distance of about two stades (approximately 400m) they come within range of the Persian archers – at this point they charge at the run through the hail of Persian archery.**

SPRIN
MA

RIVER
CHARADRA

OINOE

1

2

3

7

6

ATHENS

XXXX
Greeks
MILTIADES

MARATHON

N

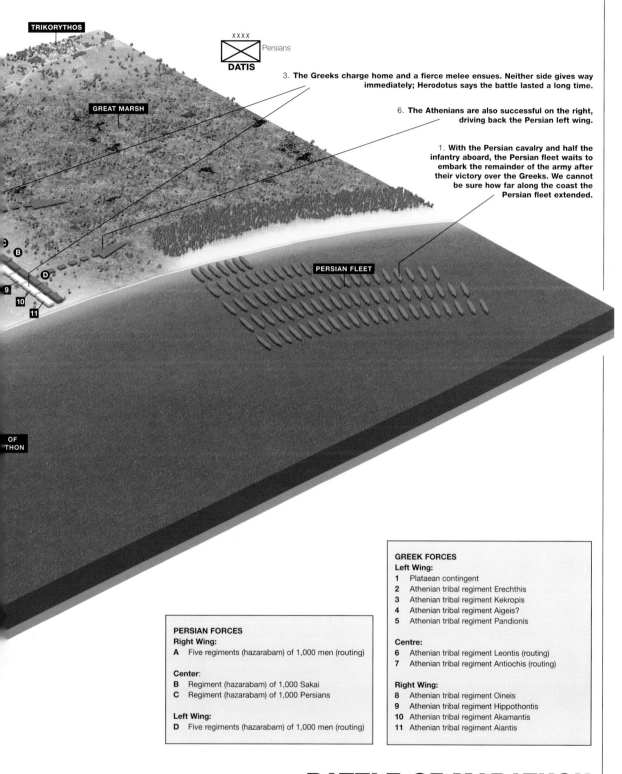

TRIKORYTHOS

XXXX
Persians
DATIS

GREAT MARSH

3. The Greeks charge home and a fierce melee ensues. Neither side gives way immediately; Herodotus says the battle lasted a long time.

6. The Athenians are also successful on the right, driving back the Persian left wing.

1. With the Persian cavalry and half the infantry aboard, the Persian fleet waits to embark the remainder of the army after their victory over the Greeks. We cannot be sure how far along the coast the Persian fleet extended.

PERSIAN FLEET

B

D

9

10

11

OF
THON

PERSIAN FORCES
Right Wing:
A   Five regiments (hazarabam) of 1,000 men (routing)

Center:
B   Regiment (hazarabam) of 1,000 Sakai
C   Regiment (hazarabam) of 1,000 Persians

Left Wing:
D   Five regiments (hazarabam) of 1,000 men (routing)

GREEK FORCES
Left Wing:
1   Plataean contingent
2   Athenian tribal regiment Erechthis
3   Athenian tribal regiment Kekropis
4   Athenian tribal regiment Aigeis?
5   Athenian tribal regiment Pandionis

Centre:
6   Athenian tribal regiment Leontis (routing)
7   Athenian tribal regiment Antiochis (routing)

Right Wing:
8   Athenian tribal regiment Oineis
9   Athenian tribal regiment Hippothontis
10   Athenian tribal regiment Akamantis
11   Athenian tribal regiment Aiantis

BATTLE OF MARATHON
11 September 490BC, morning, viewed from the south-west, showing the Athenian charge.
The Greeks are successful on either flank but the regiments in the centre are broken

have been brought from a large radius of the surrounding surface area when the work was carried out around 460. Some earth containing old arrowheads loosened from their rotting shafts, used in the battle some 30 years earlier, would have been brought in from the scene of the Athenian charge further to the north-east.

These are the considerations upon which the written description below and the colour illustrations are based. In my opinion they make best use of the available evidence, but the reader should be warned that virtually every account of the battle written reconstructs it differently.

THE ATHENIAN CHARGE

When the line had been drawn up, and the sacrifices were favourable, the Athenians charged at a run. This is confirmed by a line in Aristophanes' play *The Acharnians* (699) which features a chorus of 'old veterans' of the deme (and tryttis) of Acharnae. They state that at Marathon 'we ran'.

Herodotus (6.112) states that no less that eight *stades* separated the the two opposing battle lines. The stade measured 600ft, giving a total distance between lines of about 1.5 kilometres. One presumes the Athenians did not run the whole of this distance, but only the part when they would be within the range of Persian archery. McLeod (1970) has gathered the evidence for ancient bow ranges which suggests that bows at this period were effective up to 'at least 160-175 metres, but not as far as 350–450 metres'. Therefore the Greeks would have had to run for at least 200 or even 300m sustaining casualties from the arrows. Justin (2.9) mistakenly states that the Athenians started their run 1,000 paces (a little more than four stades or 750m) from the enemy.

The charge at the run had been introduced as a tactic into several Greek armies who predicted they might have to charge through Persian archery. The run in armour (*hoplitodromos*) was also introduced as an

A hoplite charge at the run is shown on this Attic black-figure amphora painted some ten years or so before Marathon. It demonstrates that the tactic was commonplace. Here two ranks are shown in the charge. (Munich, Museum für Antike Kleinkunst 1510)

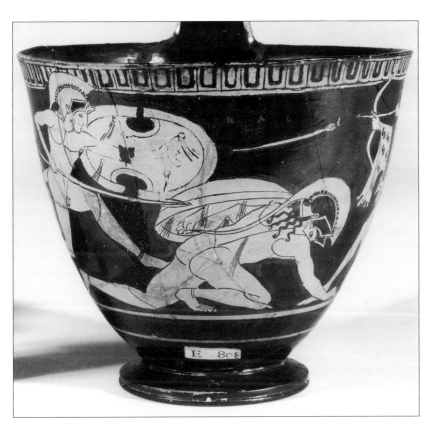

athletic competition and, at the same time, to train hoplites for running in armour. It was included as an event in the Olympic Games from 520, and in the Pythian Games from 498, originally run over a distance of two stades (about 360m). It seems the hoplite would not be expected to run futher than this distance, and that they began their charge at the run two stades away from the Persian line. Indeed, this is precisely when, according to McLeod's evidence, they would have first come within effective range of the Persian archery. Runners in the *hoplitodromos* were equipped with shield, helmet and greaves, but with no cuirass. The wearing of greaves was discontinued after 450. One might assume from this that once the decision to deliver the charge at a run had been taken, the Athenian hoplites would have left their cuirasses behind in the camp at the Herakleion, and fought without them. However the hoplites on the Oxford Brygos cup do wear cuirasses.

According to Herodotus (6.112) the Persians thought the Greeks had been struck mad when they saw their small numbers and them advancing at a run without support of cavalry or archers. It has been claimed that the source for this statement was a Persian prisoner (Whatley 135), or one of the Greeks accompanying Hippias (Avery 1972, 15 n. 2), but it is more likely that this is simply what the Greeks imagined was passing through the minds of their enemies.

The mêlée

When the Athenian line struck that of the Persians the result of the battle was not decided instantly. 'We may reasonably suppose that [the charge had] disordered the Athenian ranks, and that when they reached the

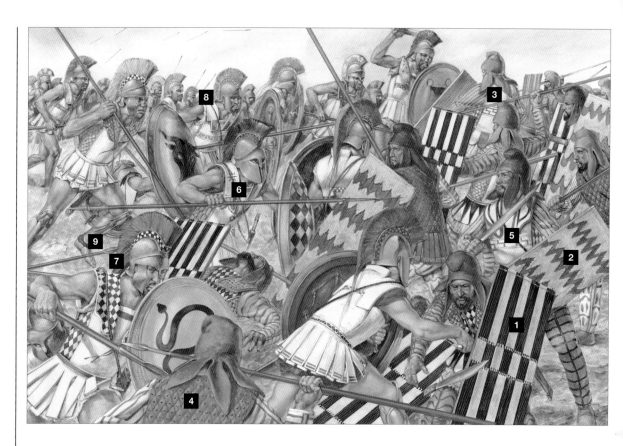

THE ATHENIAN CHARGE REACHES THE PERSIAN LINE
(pages 66–67)

The Persian infantry regiments were organised in a decimal system, and would have been drawn up ten ranks deep. The file of ten men (*dathabam*) was commanded by a decurion (*dathpati?*) who would stand in the front of the file armed with a spear and a pavise (*spara*). These troops, *sparabara*, drew their shields together into a shield-wall, from behind which the other nine ranks of archers in the file would shoot. All the Persians shown here are *sparabarai*, and all are based on the three figures of Persians show on the Oxford Brygos cup. There is a considerable amount of evidence for regimental uniform in the Achaemenid army. Consequently we have taken the opportunity to show three repeated sets of dress and equipment. In fact if the different Persian regiments were dressed uniformly one would not find the members of three different regiments mixed up like this. The majority of figures carry a *spara* (1) based on that shown on the Oxford Brygos cup although others carry a *spara* of different construction based on examples recovered by archaeological excavation (2). The majority of the Persians wear composite cuirasses of a type quite close to the Greek equivalent with which we are familiar (3). In fact it seems probable that the Greek composite cuirass

was inspired by oriental prototypes. Other Persians wear a different type of cuirass (4) reminiscent of the mediaeval 'jack' in appearance, and presumably of a similar construction. Some of the *sparabara* have lost their spears and fight with swords of the *kopis* type (5). In contrast the Athenians are of a much more varied appearance. Unlike the mercenaries fighting on the Achaemenid side, each Athenian citizen was responsible for supplying his own equipment. Thus we find the hoplites wearing helmets of Corinthian (6), Attic (7), and even Illyrian (8) types. Similarly there is no uniformity among the devices they bear on their shields. By and large the composite cuirass had replaced the muscle cuirass by the time of Marathon. It is possible that the Athenians left their cuirasses and greaves behind in camp once the decision had been made to charge the Persian line at the run. However there is no positive evidence to support this supposition, and indeed late Archaic vases show hoplites charging at the run in full armour. It was common practice at this period to wear 'garters' underneath the bottom edge of the greave to prevent chaffing of the skin (9). These would have been even more necessary at Marathon than was normally the case if the Athenian hoplites ran several hundred metres in greaves. (Richard Hook)

Persian front, they were both out of breath and unsteady' (Grote 276). Herodotus (6.113) tells us that the battle went on for a long time. Greek hoplite battles were usually decided very quickly, in a matter of minutes rather than hours. In fact the lines frequently did not come into contact. At Marathon both sides decided to stand and fight. After their spears were broken the Greeks and Persians continued to fight with their swords (Aristoph., *Knights* 781). A number of stories are preserved of supernatural visions experienced by the soldiers fighting at Marathon.

Herodotus (6.117) records that Epizelos son of Kouphagoras lost his sight in the middle of the action, while fighting bravely. He had suffered barely a scratch on his body, but was struck blind from that day on until the end of his life. Herodotus says that Epizelos 'used to say' that he saw confronting him a huge hoplite whose beard covered his whole shield. This spectre passed by him but killed the man standing at his side. Plutarch (*Mor.* 305B) gives a garbled version of the same story. Evidently Epizelos sufferered a psychosomatic trauma brought on by the physical and mental stress of battle.

Herodotus chose to omit numerous stories of supernatural aid afforded to the Athenians which were in circulation in his day. He may fail to record them either because he thinks they were later accretions to the Marathon legend (How & Welles 354) or because he simply did not believe them (Garland 55). Plutarch (*Theseus* 35) says that many of those who fought at Marathon thought they saw an apparition of the Athenian hero Theseus in arms rushing on in front of them against the enemy. This detail could well be a later fabrication of the Kimonian propaganda campaign. The legend of Echetlos, recorded by Pausanias (1.32.5) is more difficult to explain in this way. In the fighting there appeared a man dressed in country clothes and of rustic appearance, who slaughtered many of the Persians with a plough, but who was never

Demosthenes (59. 94) states that the Plataeans shown in the painting of Marathon in the Painted Stoa were recognizable by their Boeotian helmets. The Boeotian helmet copied the shape of the wide-brimmed Boeotian felt hat. The only preserved helmets of this type date to the 4th century. However this representation carved in stone could be 5th century in date. (Peter Fraser)

seen again after the battle. After the battle the Athenians consulted the oracle at Delphi and Apollo ordered them to worship Echetlaios 'He of the Plough-handle' as a hero. Aelian (*NA* 6.38) tells us that one Athenian had his dog with him at the battle, which appears in the painting of the battle in the Painted Stoa.

In the centre the Persians won, for this was where they had stationed their best troops – the Persian and Saka regiments. The Persians may have been spearmen more suitably equipped for hand-to-hand fighting than the archers and pavise-bearers on the two flanks of the line. They were also fighting against the weakened tribes of the centre of the Athenian line. Plutarch (*Arist.* 5.3) mentions that it was the two tribes Leontis and Antiochis which were hardest pressed. If drawn up 4 deep they would be occupying a frontage of 450 files, fighting approximately four or five Persian regiments drawn up 10 deep. Plutarch says that it was here that the Persian line held longest, while Herodotus says that the Persians actually won, they broke the Athenian line 'and pursued them inland' (towards Agrieliki). As has already been suggested, the two broken regiments may have only been able to rally in the area of the Sorós.

On the wings the Athenians and Plataeans were victorious and routed their enemy. It may have been the Plataeans who first broke the Persian line at its extreme right flank, given that the *tropaion* or trophy of weapons [which was traditionally built at the point where the battle 'turned'] was later built around this area. Pausanias (1.32.7) states that when the Persian line broke, many of the barbarians fell into the lake and the marshes because of their ignorance of the paths through it, and that this was the cause of their great losses. His evidence is supported by Pausanias (1.15.3) who records that the centre of the picture in the

Although painted 30 years after the battle, the bull's head on the hoplite's shield may be intended to mark him as a veteran of Marathon. He wears a Boeotian helmet, and so may be one of the Plataeans fighting on the left wing. He stabs a Persian archer between the shoulder-piece and breast-plate of his cuirass with his spear. One the other side of the vase a second archer runs, panic-stricken, into the Great Marsh. (Antikenmuseum Basel und Sammlung Ludwig, Inv. BS 480 photo: Claire Niggli)

Painted Stoa showed the barbarians in flight and pushing one another into the morass.

In a confusing passage Herodotus (6.113) records that that the two wings of the Athenian line allowed their routed enemy to flee, joined the two wings together, and fought the enemy who had broken their centre. Does Herodotus mean the Athenians about-faced in formed units, formed a new line and then advanced inland against the Persian centre? A manoeuvre as complicated as this would be beyond the training of Greek troops of this period. Perhaps he is describing an action altogether less complicated and formal. Perhaps groups streamed back on their own initiative to hit the Persian centre in rear? Either way the Athenians were victorious. As the Persians fled, the Greeks followed them, cutting them down until they reached the sea.

The battle by the ships

Fighting now took place on the shoreline where the last Persian ships were 'backing out' to sea (Hdt. 6.115). The tribe Aiantis was most heavily involved in the fighting. As Aiantis was stationed on the extreme right of the Athenian line, this would seem to confirm that the two lines were formed up and fought at right angles to the coast, and not parallel to it. We may assume that the Persian fleet had remained at anchor along the whole 3km length of Schoinias beach while it awaited the outcome of the battle so as to pick up the remainder of their forces. The fighting for the ships would have taken place at the very south-west end of the beach, not far behind the original position of the Persian left wing, before the Persian ships had time to put to sea.

The interior of the Oxford Brygos cup shows two middle-aged, bearded warriors rising from a common tomb. The moulding indicates an altar. They stand back-to-back, unsheathing their swords for action. It has been suggested that they may represent two Marathonian heroes rising from their grave to defend Athens once again, presumably at Plataea. Presumably these two heroes are the only two officers who died, the Polemarch Kallimachos and the *strategos* Stesileos, who fell in the fighting near the ships.

Kallimachos the Polemarch now fell 'having proved himself a good man and true' (Hdt. 6.114). Plutarch (*Mor.* 305B) says that the body of Kallimachos was pierced with so many spears that although dead, he stood upright. The *strategos* Stesileos son of Thrasileos, presumably of Aiantis, also fell (Hdt. 6.114). The Athenians 'called for fire and laid hold of the ships'. There was little point calling for fire, as the nearest

The battle by the ships is shown on this Roman sarcophagus. On the right Persians attempt to drag their wounded aboard ship, in the centre Aischylos holds his dying brother Kynegeiros in his arms, on the left a Persian is pulled from his horse. The ferocity of the fighting is shown on the left, where an unarmed Persian bites the leg of an Athenian hoplite, and a horseman (an officer?) is dragged from his mount. (Brescia Archaeological Museum)

fire available was miles away in the Athenian camp. The battle had now reached the level of an epic struggle, and the similarity with the Homeric battle by the ships would have surely not been lost on the contemporary participants. 'Herodotus in describing this incident is at his most Homeric, unconsciously equating it with the great moment when Hector laid hands on the ships of the Achaeans and called for fire (*Il.* 15. 718)' (J.R. Grant, *Phoenix* 23 (1969) 264).

Kynegeiros son of Euphorion, gripped the poop of one of the Persian ships with his hand and had it chopped off with an axe: he died, as did 'many renowned Athenians also'. The loss of a hand might not prove fatal in modern warfare, but the ancients lacked the means to replace large quantities of lost blood. Kynegeiros must have bled to death. He probably died in the sight, and arms, of his brother Aischylos. Justin (2.9) records an embroidered version of Kynegeiros' heroism at the ships, where he first loses his right hand, but then grabs hold of the ship with his left hand. When this is cut off in turn he grabs hold of the ship with his teeth! According to Justin he 'fought to the last, maimed as he was, with his teeth, like a wild beast'. Justin fails to explain how he managed to keep hold of the ship with his teeth and fight with them at the same time.

The Athenians succeeded in capturing seven Persian ships. Pausanias (1.15.3) states that the end of the picture in the Painted Stoa showed the Phoenician ships, and the Greeks killing the foreigners scrambling into them. It seems the Athenians killed a considerable number of the enemy as they were boarding the triremes. Ktesias (18) states that Datis was among the dead, and that the Athenians refused to give up his body. He is surely mistaken, for Herodotus mentions Datis having a dream later on at the island of Mykonos. Cicero (*ad Atticum* 9.10.3) followed by Justin (2.9) says that Hippias also died in the battle, but once again this seems to be false information for both Ktesias (18) and Suidas (*Hippias* 2) say he died later on the island of Lemnos.

The epic battle fought by the Trojans for the Greek ships, here defended by the hero Ajax, is recorded in the 15th book of Homer's *Iliad* and is shown in this scene from an amphora. Grote (277) remarked that the fighting by the ships 'must have emphatically recalled' this work in the mind of the tragic poet Aischylos. (Munich, Museum für Antike Kleinkunst 3171 - J. 890)

The shield signal

Herodotus (6.115) records that 'there was a slander prevalent in Athens' that the Persians got the idea of their surprise attack on Athens from a sign sent to them by the Alkmaeonids. 'It was said' that the Alkmaeonids, in accordance with a pact with the Persians, showed a signal, holding up a shield, for the Persians aboard the ships. It should be noted that Herodotus clearly states that the traitors held up a shield, not flashed a signal from it. Indeed a signal cannot physically be flashed from the convex surface of a hoplite shield (Hodge 2001).

Herodotus goes to great lengths to defend the Alkmaeonids from the treason charge, even though he states there is no doubt a shield was shown (6.124). Despite Herodotus' kind

Ostrakon cast against Kallixenos son of Aristonymos the Alkmaeonid with a broken inscription, apparently naming him a *prodotes* or 'traitor'. He is our best candidate for the leader of the pro-Persian conspiracy in Athens. (American School of Classical Studies at Athens: Agora Excavations Inv. P. 3786)

2. Groups of Athenian troops from the left and right wings turn back and successfully attack the Persians and Sakai in the rear. It is uncertain in what direction the Persians fled.

3. The broken Athenian regiments Antiochis and Leontis, may have rallied in the area where the Soros was later erected. After resting and reforming they were left on the battlefield to collect the Athenian dead. This may explain why the burial of the Athenian dead took place here. It seems unlikely that the Persian centre pushed this far inland or that any heavy fighting took place in this area.

SPRI
MA

RIVER
CHARADRA

OINOE

ATHENS

B
C
B

6 7

MARATHON

XXXX
Greeks
MILTIADES

N

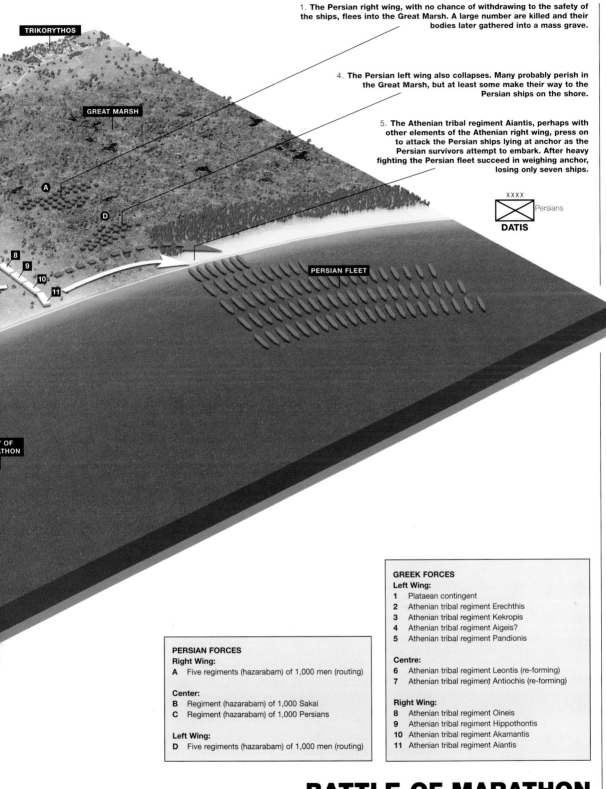

TRIKORYTHOS

1. The Persian right wing, with no chance of withdrawing to the safety of the ships, flees into the Great Marsh. A large number are killed and their bodies later gathered into a mass grave.

4. The Persian left wing also collapses. Many probably perish in the Great Marsh, but at least some make their way to the Persian ships on the shore.

5. The Athenian tribal regiment Aiantis, perhaps with other elements of the Athenian right wing, press on to attack the Persian ships lying at anchor as the Persian survivors attempt to embark. After heavy fighting the Persian fleet succeed in weighing anchor, losing only seven ships.

GREAT MARSH

A

D

8
9
10
11

PERSIAN FLEET

XXXX

Persians

DATIS

Y OF THON

PERSIAN FORCES
Right Wing:
A   Five regiments (hazarabam) of 1,000 men (routing)

Center:
B   Regiment (hazarabam) of 1,000 Sakai
C   Regiment (hazarabam) of 1,000 Persians

Left Wing:
D   Five regiments (hazarabam) of 1,000 men (routing)

GREEK FORCES
Left Wing:
1   Plataean contingent
2   Athenian tribal regiment Erechthis
3   Athenian tribal regiment Kekropis
4   Athenian tribal regiment Aigeis?
5   Athenian tribal regiment Pandionis

Centre:
6   Athenian tribal regiment Leontis (re-forming)
7   Athenian tribal regiment Antiochis (re-forming)

Right Wing:
8   Athenian tribal regiment Oineis
9   Athenian tribal regiment Hippothontis
10   Athenian tribal regiment Akamantis
11   Athenian tribal regiment Aiantis

BATTLE OF MARATHON
11 September 490BC, viewed from the south-west, showing the destruction of the Persian forces and the fighting around the ships.

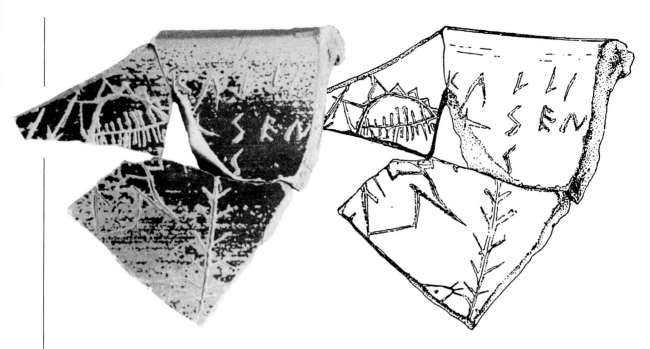

A second ostrakon cast against
Kallixenos son of Aristonymos
also includes an 'unflattering
portrait' of the 'traitor'.
(American School of Classical
Studies at Athens: Agora
Excavations Inv. P. 7103)

words, the Alkmaeonids undoubtedly formed a 'fifth column' in Athens, serving Hippias and the Persians. The person who showed the shield was probably Kallixenos son of Aristonymos the Alkmaeonid (Bicknell 434 n. 57); his name appears on a huge number of ostraka of the 480s, and on one he is called 'the traitor'. Another Alkmaeonid traitor may have been Megakles son of Hippokrates, ostracized in 487/86, when, as Aristotle (*Ath. Pol.* 22. 6) tells us, the Athenians started to ostracize 'the friends of the tyrants' which continued for three years.

The signal must have had a simple pre-arranged meaning. Most modern authorities maintain that it was a sign that Athens was ripe for a coup, and that the Persians could now make their move. This is illogical, given that the signal came after the Persians had already started to embark. It has been suggested that on the contrary, the signal communicated that the plot had failed. Indeed, the later confusion that developed in Athens as to whether or not the Alkmaeonids were traitors 'is far more easily explained if their conspiracy had failed to materialise' (Reynolds 102–3). At this stage a key factor in Persian operational planning was the activity of the Lakedaimonian army – had it left yet, and when would it arrive at Athens? It may have been information on this subject that was transmitted by the signal.

Datis decided the capture of Athens while unguarded had to be attempted. The Athenian army would have been exhausted and disorganized after the battle, and might take a long time to get back to the city before the Persian fleet arrived. Could the Athenians risk a second battle in their exhausted and depleted state? Although the Athenians lost only 192 dead (Hdt. 6.117) 'total casualties must have been at least five times that number, one tribe probably remained on the field of battle, and it is nowhere stated that the Plataeans came back to Athens; moreover, it had fought a hard battle and done a forced march since morning, and must have been utterly tired out, while the Persians in the ships were fresh' (Reynolds 102).

THE RACE TO PHALERON

The main Persian fleet in Marathon Bay backed water, sailed to the island of Aigilia to collect the Eretrian captives, and then sailed on towards Cape Sounion. According to Herodotus (6.115) they hoped to reach Athens before the Athenian army.

There has been much debate as to how long it might take the Persian fleet to get to Phaleron. The distance around Cape Sounion from Marathon to Phaleron is around 100km, and the latest estimates indicate that a single trireme could have covered this distance, optimistically, in about 10 hours (Lazenby 74). Ten years later the Persian fleet took three days to reach Phaleron from the Euripus straits of Euboea (Hdt. 8.66), but they were in no hurry, and the weather conditions are unknown.

Plutarch (*Arist.* 5. 4) states that when the Athenians had pushed the Persians back into their ships, they saw that they were sailing not back towards the Cyclades, but were being 'forced back by an onshore wind and swell towards Attica'. In other words there was a strong wind and high seas were running towards Cape Sounion. This wind Plutarch describes would seem to be the wind known to the ancients as the Etesian and to the moderns as Meltemi, a seasonal wind which blows into early September (Hodge 1975, 99).

Calculation of the journey time is more complicated. Had part of the fleet already left, perhaps even the day before? Were they sailing with only their fastest ships, or accompanied by slower transports? What were the weather conditions? It has escaped modern commentators that these questions would also have been asked by the Athenians as they saw the Persian fleet back out. It was imperative to get back to the city as soon as possible, assuming, of course, that the Persians had not already reached Athens!

According to a number of late sources a messenger was sent ahead first to take news of the victory to Athens. According to Plutarch (*Mor.* 347C) Herakleides Pontikos stated that it was Thersippos of Eroidai, but most historians say it was Eukles who ran to the city 'in full armour'. He died at the doors of the government buildings having only been able to shout out 'Hail, we are victorious!'. Lucian (*Pro Lapsu* 3) says it was Philippides who brought the news to the archons, shouted 'Joy to you, we've won,' and died. Given these conflicting accounts, Frost (1979) has suggested that no messenger was sent back at all.

The land route was slightly less than the distance of the modern Marathon run (which was extended for the second London Olympics so as to pass beneath the balconies of Buckingham Palace) – a demanding march for an already exhausted army. Herodotus (6.113) states that the battle had lasted 'a long time': just how long is difficult to say. It must have taken a massive effort on the part of the commanders to get the tired troops reorganized after the battle and set them on the march. According to Frontinus (*Strat.* 2.9.8) it was Miltiades who halted their rejoicing and set them on the march back. The Athenian army 'rushing with all speed to defend their city' (Hdt. 6.116), reached it before the Persian fleet and encamped in the sanctuary of Herakles at Kynosarges, a suburb of Athens. Most modern historians maintain the Athenian army arrived on the evening of the day of the battle, which seems

THE ATHENIANS REACH THE HERAKLEION AT KYNOSARGES (pages 78–79)

After the battle at Marathon, which Herodotus says lasted 'a long time', the Greeks had little time to rejoice at their victory. As soon as the tired troops could be reorganised they began a forced march back to Athens, in a race against time to beat the Persian fleet to the city. Reaching Athens before the Persians, they encamped in the sanctuary of Herakles at Kynosarges. Already drained by their charge at the run and a fiercely fought battle, the forced march must have left the Athenians physically and mentally exhausted. This must have been tempered, however, by the knowledge that thanks to their Herculean efforts the city had been saved. The sanctuary of Herakles at Kynosarges lies under the modern city of Athens and very little is known of its ancient appearance at the time of Marathon. The sanctuary presumably included an extensive holy precinct (*temenos*) surrounding the temple itself, big enough to hold the Athenian forces. This quite possibly included a sacred grove of olives (1). Night has fallen, but the scene is illuminated by the moon of the lunar month *Metageitnion*, which has only just started to wane (2). The cult statue of Herakles (3) is based on an Archaic bronze now in Kassel. It may originally have been a Lakonian work, and may copy the cult statue of Herakles in armour from the Spartan Sanctuary of Herakles mentioned by Pausanias (3.15.3). We have no comparable representational evidence of this type from Athens. The armour worn by the Athenian hoplites is largely of composite type, and our re-constructions are largely based on information from the Oxford Brygos cup and the lost vase once on the Rome market. Notice the shield lying flat to the bottom left of the picture (4), which copies one shown on p.19. The diamond pattern surface decoration of the shield might reflect that it too was of composite construction. The figure to right of centre (5) is particularly worthy of attention as it attempts to recreate the figure shown on p.18. Note the bronze scales of the upper back plate fixed to run upwards, and the composite helmet. The skull is made of plates fixed to an outer shell of hardened leather by ornamental rivets. To his right stands a hoplite (6) based on one of the figures shown on p.44. The bull's head shield device is an iconographic device used to mark him out as a veteran of Marathon, as is also the Marathonian bull decorating the shield of the hoplite to his right (7). Nevertheless it is possible that these shield devices may have been used by hoplites fighting at the battle, particularly those recruited from the four settlements in the Plain of Marathon. Also shown is the *triskeles* device painted on the shield of another hoplite (8). There is some evidence to suggest that this device was particularly popular among the Alkmaeonids, who some accused of traitorous dealings with the tyrants and their Persian supporters. (Richard Hook)

probable. The forced march must have left an indelible impression in the minds of the veterans.

The Persians rounded Sounion and anchored off Phaleron. After riding at anchor for a while they sailed back to Asia. The Lakedaimonian advance party of 2,000 men arrived on the next day, 18 Metageitnion/12 September (Plato, *Laws* 698E) having set out from Sparta after the full moon and reached Athens on their third day out of the city. The total adult male population was 8,000 and the number of Spartans of fighting age at this period was 5,000. The 2,000 probably represent the first ten age-classes, sent out as a 'flying-column' to bring help as quickly as possible. Though too late for the battle, they were anxious to see what the Persians looked like, and they set off for Marathon to inspect the bodies (Hdt. 6.120). This may be when the Athenians made sketches of the clothing and equipment of the Persian dead.

Booty and burial

Aristeides had been left behind at Marathon with his tribe Antiochis 'to guard the captives and booty' (Plut., *Aristid.* 5.5–6). Plutarch says the booty was captured from the tents and the hulls of the ships. Note also that Nepos (*Milt.* 5.5) says the Persians fled, not to their camp, but to their ships. But Herodotus does not mention tents, nor any Persian

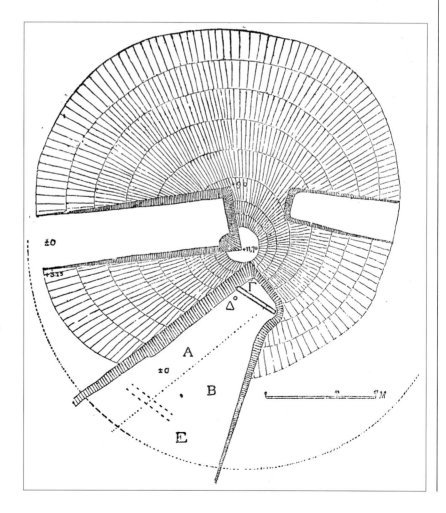

Plan of the excavations of the Sorós carried out by Valerios Staïs in 1890 and 1891, which first confirmed the identity of the tumulus as the burial place of the Athenian fallen. 'Cremation Trays' were found at points D and E, the second one being brick-lined. The latter was 5m long and 1m wide, scattered with ash, the bones of animals and birds as well as eggs consumed in the funeral feast, and intentionally smashed pottery. (*Athenische Mitteilungen* 18 (1893) 49)

One of the few remaining wetland areas left on the Marathon plain, just behind the Megalo-Mati pumping station. This gives an idea of the marshes into which many of the defeated Persians fled and where they met their deaths.

camp. My assumption is the Persians had broken camp the previous night when the bulk of their forces had embarked. The booty was taken from the captured ships and from enemy bodies and captives. References to the Persian camp and tents were probably added by later authors.

Aristeides was perhaps entrusted with this task because of his reputation for honesty. Herodotus (8.79.1) made enquiries into Aristeides' character and was 'convinced that he was the best and justest man in Athens'. He was elected eponymous archon for the following year 489/88. (It is also possible that his tribe Antiochis was left behind because it had suffered most in the battle.) Plutarch says Aristeides allowed nobody to touch the booty. It was pooled communally, and the Plataeans were later given their share (Paus. 9.4.1).

Fighting in the ranks of Antiochis was Aristeides' cousin, Kallias son of Hipponikos of the deme Alopeke, who was hereditary torchbearer in the Eleusinian mysteries. Kallias was extremely wealthy, so much so that his nickname was *Lakkoploutos* 'well-wealthy'. The nickname surely only means that his wealth was 'as deep as a well'. However, malicious gossips invented a story of how he had acquired his wealth. He had fought in the battle in priestly dress. A Persian placed himself under his protection and showed Kallias where he had buried money in a well (*lakkos*). Kallias killed the Persian and took the money. A more plausible explanation of the family's wealth is given by Herakleides Pontikos (Athenaeus 12.537A). An Eretrian named Diomnestos gave his riches to Kallias' father for safe-keeping. When Diomnestos was deported with the other Eretrians, Hipponikos kept the money.

Another duty of the Antiochis regiment would have been to bury the dead. The burial of the Athenian dead on the field of battle was quite exceptional. Thucydides (2.34.5) and Pausanias state that the normal practice was to bring the remains of the fallen back to the city, and that this exception was due to the 'outstanding valour' of those who fought at Marathon. They were awarded heroic honours: Pausanias(1.32.4) says a cult was established. An annual sacrifice was performed at the Sorós under the auspices of the Polemarch 'on behalf of those who had died in the cause of freedom' (Garland 58).

Herodotus (6.117) gives the number of dead as 192 Athenians (not including Plataeans or slaves) and 6,400 Persians. Most historians have accepted this figure because they think it reasonable or believe a body count was made after the battle. Yet the ratio of dead 1:33⅓ looks suspicious (Avery 1973). According to Justin (2.9) the Persians lost 2,000 men in the battle and shipwrecks. If we combine the variant traditions dealing with how it came about that 500 goats were sacrificed to Artemis Agrotera, a case could be made for 500 barbarian casualties. Pausanias says the Athenians insist that they buried the Persian dead, because, he (1.32.5) states 'in every case the divine law applies that a corpse should be laid under the earth, yet I could find no grave. There was neither mound nor other trace to be seen, as the dead were carried to a trench and thrown in anyhow'.

In the winter of 1884/5 Captain von Eschenburg surveyed the Marathon Plain to produce an archaeological map of the area. He records that 'in the vineyard belonging to Skouzes a large quantity of remains of bones was found, haphazardly placed, which seems to belong to hundreds of dead. I thank for the information Mr. Skouzes' steward, a clever young Greek under whose direction the vineyard was planted. I myself dug at the edges of the vineyard and ascertained that this area full of remains of bones extends as far as the marshes' (Petrakos 24). Most agree that von Eschenburg had found the Persian mass grave. Presumably it never had any monumental superstructure, hence Pausanias' inability to find it. The location, between the Church of Panaghia Mesosporitisa and the Great Marsh, would fit what we know of the battle, for the majority of the Persians seem to have died in the Marsh.

An interesting piece of trivia is connected with the battle. Pliny (*HN* 18.43.144) states that 'Median Grass', lucerne or alfalfa, is foreign to Greece and was first brought from Media (its place of origin) 'during the Persian war which Darius launched'. It has been suggested that the occasion was Marathon; the grass perhaps was self-seeding (Evans 103). If Marathon was the occasion, the grass was more likely found as fodder in one of the seven captured triremes. A more likely opportunity for the arrival of 'Median Grass' was the wreck of the Persian fleet off Mount Athos in 492. This was the occasion when, for example, white pigeons first came to Europe (L. Pearson, *Early Ionian Historians* 147–8).

AFTERMATH

Datis sailed back to Asia via the island of Mykonos, and there had a vision in his sleep. At dawn he searched his ships and found a golden image of Apollo in one of the Phoenician vessels. He asked where this image had been looted, and after learning the name of the shrine, he sailed with his own ship to Delos. There he placed the image in the shrine of Apollo and asked the Delians to take the image to the sanctuary of Delion in Theban territory on the coast opposite Chalkis. The Delians failed to comply with his request. It was only some 20 years later, on the command of a prophecy, that the Thebans took the statue to Delion (Hdt. 6.118).

Immediately after the battle the Athenians consecrated a temple to Eukleia 'Glory' from the spoils of the battle (Paus. 1.14.5). They also started construction work on the predecessor of the Parthenon. A cave under the Acropolis was dedicated to Pan and sacrifices and torch-races in his honour were intiated. The votive statue of Pan was supposedly inscribed with an epigram by Simonides: 'Me, the goatfooted Pan, the Arcadian, hostile to Medes, to the Athenians an aid, Miltiades erected'. Pan was worshipped in a number of caves throughout Attica. There is no evidence for such worship at any of these sites prior to the battle, nor does the god appear in Attic art before that date. Garland (61) believes there was a dramatic expansion in the god's cult after 490, rather than a completely fresh start.

Limestone head of Pan, 0.354m high, once painted in colour, of which traces remain. It is said to have been found on the north slope of the Acropolis, and so would seem to be a fragment of statue dedicated before the Persian sack of 480/79. A cult statue as important as the one dedicated by Miltiades would probably have been of bronze, not stone. (Cleveland Museum of Art 26. 538)

Soon after the Marathon campaign, the Athenians granted Miltiades a fleet of 70 ships to make war on the islands that had helped the Persians. Some date the expedition to immediately after Marathon, as the Parians believed that Datis was still at Mykonos with his fleet. Others place the campaign in 489. According to Nepos (1.7) Miltiades compelled many of the islands to change sides, but the Parians refused, confident in their fortifications. He laid siege to the city and demanded 100 talents compensation. Herodotus (6.134) says that several differing accounts of events had survived. The Parians claimed that a priestess named Timo was showing Miltiades a way into the city when he injured his thigh in trying to leap over a fence. In another account Ephoros says the Parians were on the point of surrender when a chance fire broke out on Mykonos. They assumed it was Datis and the Persian fleet signalling to them, so they continued to resist. After 26 days the siege was lifted.

On his return to Athens Miltiades was prosecuted on the capital charge of 'deceiving the Athenian people' by an Alkmaeonid, Xanthippos son of Ariphron. Unable to stand, he was defended by his friends. His wound had started to putrify, and he was confined to a couch. Miltiades escaped the death sentence, but was fined the enormous sum of 50 talents (300,000 drachmas). He died in prison soon after with the fine still unpaid, and his son Kimon was left to settle the debt.

The cult of Pan was established in this cave on the north-west slope of the Acropolis. The role of Pan in the battle is puzzling. The 2nd century BC historian Polemon (2.41) refers to one of the Persian ships 'being pursued by Pan'. Julius Africanus (*Kestai* 1.2.11) says that Pan fought against the Persians at Marathon alongside the Athenians. Aristeides (*Panath.* 108 [202D]) writing in the 2nd century AD mentions the 'dance of Pan' being performed after the battle. Strangely, Pan does not participate in the battle either in Herodotus' account or in the painting of the battle in the Painted Stoa.

When the Persian fleet reached Asia, Datis and Artaphernes took the enslaved Eretrians to Susa. Despite the damage they had done to his property (the city of Sardis) Darius did them no further harm, but settled them on his own estates at Arderikka in Cissia 'and they were there in that country still in my time, still speaking their ancient language' records Herodotus (6.199). No more is heard of Datis. Whether he was executed for his failure, as Plato suggests, is unknown. Nine years later Xerxes led a second invasion of Greece with Mardonios commanding the army. Nepos (*Pausanias* 1) states that Mardonios was 'the royal satrap, by nation a Mede'. If, as discussed earlier, this designation relates to office rather than nationality, Mardonios may have also replaced Datis as satrap of Media.

To some extent the glory of the battle of Marathon was diminished by the victories won over the Persians a decade later. Many of the monuments and festivals associated with Marathon were established much later thanks to the activities of Kimon, son of Miltiades, who rose to political prominence in the 460s. Perhaps the most famous of these was the painting of the battle of Marathon by Mikon and Panainos in the 'Painted Stoa' at Athens. In this painting Miltiades took pride of place among the other heroes of the battle (Paus. 1.15.3). Probably it was only in the Kimonian period too that the Sorós was piled over the grave of the fallen. Likewise we do not know if the cult of the Marathonian heroes was established immediately after the battle, or grew up later, especially in the period of Kimon.

The celebration of the battle took place not on the anniversary of the battle – 17 Metageitnion (11 September) – but on 6 Boedromion, the festival of Artemis Agroteria, to whom the Athenians had offered to sacrifice before the battle. The battle was still being commemorated at least 367 years later, and possibly much longer still after that (Petrakos 38–9).

Kimonian propaganda also exalted Miltiades and Marathon at the pan-Hellenic shrine at Delphi. Pausanias (10.10.1–2) describes a series of statues showing the Athenian tribal and other heroes, plus Athena,

This vase, found in the debris of the Persian sack of Athens in 480/79, might have been 'specially dedicated at what might well have been a sanctuary of Zeus Eleutherios in memory of the victory of Marathon' (Williams 78 n. 33). A warrior, perhaps personifying Kallimachos, pours a libation at the altar of Zeus 'God of Freedom'. After the Persian Wars the sanctuary of Zeus the 'Saviour' at Athens was given the further name 'Liberator'. (Athens, American School of Classical Studies, Agora Excavations P 42)

Lebes (cauldron) in the Canellopoulos Collection, discovered around 1958 near the Sorós, it reputedly contained charred human bones when found. The inscription around the rim runs 'The Athenians (give this as) a prize (in the games) for those (who died) in the war'. It was probably won in the games established by the Athenians to honour the dead at Marathon as heroes. (Athens, Canellopoulos Museum 199)

Apollo and Miltiades. He says that the statues were by Pheidias, and that an inscription recorded that they were a tithe of the spoils taken at Marathon. This is impossible. Pheidias was too young to have produced the statues; he was active only in the middle of the century, during the administrations of Kimon and Perikles. For the same reasons Pheidias' statue of Athena Promachos on the Acropolis cannot have been made from a tithe of the booty of the battle, as Pausanias (1.28.2) asserts.

Another false inscription runs around the base of the Athenian Treasury at Delphi, proclaiming 'The Athenians dedicate to Apollo the tenth of the booty they took from the Medes during the battle of Marathon'. Pausanias (10.11.5) accordingly believed that the Treasury had been built from the spoils of Marathon. In fact the Treasury seems to have been built before Marathon, and the inscribed base was added later. Great care is needed when considering what light these monuments can actually shed on the battle.

The democratic Athens that had taken shape over the 17 years that had passed since the reforms of Kleisthenes was a very different society from the faction-torn Athens of the days of Peisistratos (Reynolds 103). It is doubtful that Hippias would have really been able to bring about the betrayal of anything other than a limited minority in the city. This was perhaps the biggest shortcoming in Persian strategic and operational planning.

On a tactical level, it must be remembered that Greeks and Persians had not yet really encountered one another in battle, and had no preconceived opinions as to the relative merits of their different equipment and methods of fighting. According to Herodotus (6.112)

the Athenians at Marathon were the first Greeks to have charged the enemy at a run, and were the first to endure the sight of Median dress and the men that wore it: 'for up till then even the name of the Medes was a terror for the Greeks'. This last statement needs a little correction, for the eastern Greeks had the dubious pleasure of fighting Persians during the Ionian Revolt.

Undoubtedly the Athenians and Plataeans had displayed great resolve in daring to face the Persians, and dauntless courage in the battle. But had the Athenian commander responsible for the deployment, be it Kallimachos or Miltiades, thinned the centre merely because of their numerical inferiority and their fear of being outflanked? Or had he deliberately sought the repulse of the Athenian centre? Was the aim of the deployment to provoke a double envelopment along the lines of Cannae as so many military historians assert? Or had they been forced to thin the line where it stood least chance of causing complete defeat.

Two considerations prevent us from making a decision. We have no idea of whether the victorious Athenians on the wings turned to attack the Persian centre deployed in tactical formations. Nothing supports such a view. We have no other description of a Greek hoplite army being capable of such sophisticated manoeuvre this early on, and there is no indication in any of our sources that any of the Greeks predicted the collapse of their centre. They probably turned back on the Persians and Sakai in the centre in 'huddles'. On the other hand it is true that Miltiades had some experience of Persian methods of warfare. If he knew that the Persians would station their commander and their best forces in the centre of the line, why then did he deploy the weakest Athenian forces at precisely this point?

The Sorós at Marathon. The mound was probably erected over the graves of the Athenian dead two decades or more after the battle, when Kimon's propaganda campaign to celebrate the battle was at its height. The mound today, decapitated by the initial primitive excavations of Schliemann and two and a half millennia of erosion, still rises some 9m above the present ground surface and has a diameter of 50m. Staïs established that the ancient surface of the plain lies some 3m further down, so the Sorós was originally at least 12m high. Soil must have been brought from an extensive surface area of the surrounding plain for its construction.

VISITING THE BATTLEFIELD

The distances across the plain of Marathon on the map seem much greater when you are walking them under a September sun. I would advise any visitor to the battlefield to hire a car, but the following short guide is for anyone travelling by public transport and foot. I have given detailed directions as the terrain is so confusing.

There are many buses from Athens to Marathon, or that pass through it. One bus runs all the way to ΣΧΟΙΝΙΑΣ (Schoinias) beach from Mavromateon Street. The bus stop is about 100m down from Plateia Aigyptou on the right-hand side. This bus can also be caught from the bus stop opposite the entrance to Ethniki Amyna metro station. A number of other buses from this stop, such as those marked 'Marathon', stop at Marathon Beach or the Tomb of the Athenians, a 90-minute ride. Accommodation is best found at Marathon Beach.

The lazy walker can take the bus all the way to the end of Schoinias Beach, but to walk the battlefield get off two stops after the Tomb of the Athenians. The main points of interest at Marathon are the **Frankish Tower** (site of the Trophy), the **spring of Makaria** (a survival of the Great

OPPOSITE **Remains of the old** *khâni*, **a resting place for travellers built during the Turkish period, on the road to Kato-Souli, shortly before the turn-off for Panaghia Mesosporitisa.**

BELOW **Turkish guard tower on the rocky spur above the Megalo-Mati pumping station.**

88

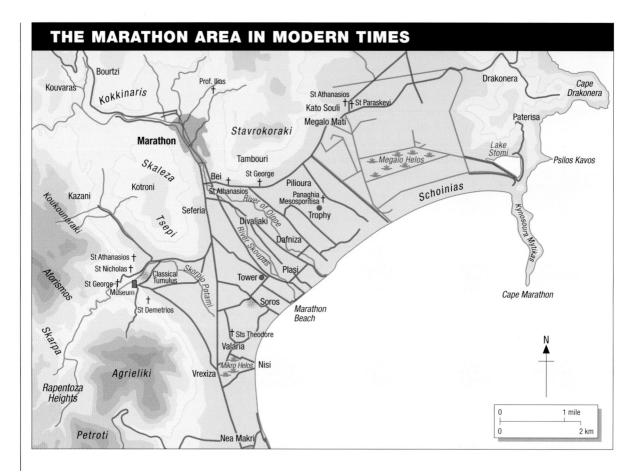

Marsh), **Schoinias Beach** (the Persian landing site and camp) and the **Museum**. The following instructions will take you to all these sites in order, but they need to be followed *very* carefully if you are not to get lost.

From the bus stop, take the road leading off east towards Schoinias and Kato Souli. Shortly after leaving the junction a modern concrete bridge crosses the course of the Charadra, in the bed of which lies a WW2 anti-tank ditch system (see photo on p.49). Continue along the road, without forking down the metalled and signposted road to the right. A spur of the Stavrokoraki mountain meets the road from the left (north). A little further on the left is the chapel of Agios Giorgios. The road now bends sharply to the left. Continue past two minor road junctions to the right, the main road continues bending left but less sharply.

A stand of tall cypresses starts running alongside the road on the right. Halfway along them are the ruins of an Ottoman period *kháni* (rest station). Carry on until the end of the cypresses then turn right (south-east) down a minor metalled road. About 15 mins from the main road, after passing a group of farmhouses and an old factory on the right, you reach a white church, which lies inside a stone enclosure wall ringed with cypress trees. The ruins of the **Frankish Tower** lie in the middle of this enclosure. Some of the chisel-decorated blocks still to be seen in the base of the Tower come from 4th-century tombs. You are now near the site of the **Trophy**.

Return to the main road and continue north-east. You come to a road junction signposted to Schoinias 2.5 km to the right (south-east).

Continue straight on to Kato Souli, the olive tree-lined road bends first left then right. On the left of the road runs a ruined stone and concrete aquaduct. Another stone aquaduct runs down to the road at right angles on the left. Ahead the road curves sharply right and then left as the spur of the mountain runs into the plain. In antiquity the **Makaria springs** rose where this mountain spur met the Great Marsh. An old Ottoman guard tower (worth a visit) can be seen on the spur above, and as you round the spur an old pumping station comes into view. The water once supplied Athens. During WW2 it was guarded by a sentry, hence the pillbox to the right of the road. To the immediate south of the pumping station is a pond. This is one of the few remaining pockets of wetland surviving the draining of the **Great Marsh**, and gives some idea of how the whole area looked in antiquity.

Return to the road junction signposted to Schoinias. It will take about half an hour to reach the south-western edge of **Schoinias Beach** walking straight along this road. In the late summer prevailing eastern winds blow onshore here, on the south-western half of the beach. It takes about an hour to walk to the north-eastern half of the beach, which is sheltered from the winds by the Kynosoura promontory. You will pass the reed-beds of the drained Schoinias marshes on the left, and then the dried-out bed of Lake Stomi. The terminus for the bus to Schoinias is at the group of restaurant buildings at the north-eastern edge of the beach.

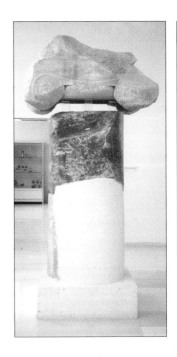

ABOVE **The surviving disjointed members of the Marathon Victory monument, the 'trophy of white marble' of Pausanias, assembled here in Marathon Museum. Many drums from the shaft are missing.**

LEFT **A Second World War pill-box on the road to Kato-Souli, 'guarding' the Megalo-Mati pumping station. Like most pill-boxes of the period, it could scarcely have been sited less effectively, commanding a view of no more than 50m.**

If you have walked for a couple of hours under the late summer sun you will now have a vague impression of the fatigue that must have been experienced by participants in the battle. Many reconstructions of the battle would have the Athenians, after charging and fighting a battle, run towards the Persian ships still anchored under Kynosoura. It is only now that you will realize the implausibility of such armchair speculation. Schoinias Beach is a fine white-sand beach, favoured by bathers from Athens, set against a backdrop of pretty umbrella pines, and is a good place for a rest.

The **Museum**, built thanks to the generosity of Evgenios Panagopoulos, a lover of archaeology, is worth a visit. At the time of writing opening hours are 8.30am to 3.00pm but the museum is closed on Mondays. The entrance ticket also gives admission to the Tomb of the Athenians. If you are walking, follow the signs to the Museum from the Marathon–Nea Makri road. You will pass the 'classical' tumulus (marked 'Tomb of the Plataeans') on the right about 200m before the museum entrance. As the Museum comes into view you will see the church of St. Demetrios slightly up on the mountainside to the left. Between you and the church is the area where Soteriades suggested the Herakleion lay. The Museum contains the Trophy monument, pottery from the 'Classical' tumulus, the two inscriptions from Valaria mentioning the cult of Herakles, all in Gallery III. Also of interest is a fine 4th-century funerary monument, a standing lion, found near the Makaria spring.

Getting back to Athens is simpler than reaching Marathon. Buses to Athens halt at stops along the main road from Marathon to Nea-Makri until quite late in the evening. In September it starts to get dark about 8.00pm.

CHRONOLOGY

499–94BC Ionian Revolt.

494BC Persian naval victory at Lade.

493BC Miltiades returns to Athens.

Persians conquer Chios, Lesbos and Tenedos.

492BC Mardonios invades Macedonia.

Persian fleet wrecked off Mount Athos.

Miltiades survives trial for tyranny and enters Athenian public life.

491BC Darius send envoys to the Greek states demanding earth and water.

Darius orders a fleet to be built and an army assembled.

490BC, early summer Datis and Artaphernes leave Darius and march to Cilicia.

July Persian fleet sets sail from Cilicia.

Siege of Lindos, Rhodes?

Persian fleets reaches Samos.

25 July Start of the Athenian civic year: Athenian generals take up office.

Early August The Persian Campaign in the Cyclades.

22 August Panathenaic Games. Victory of Kallimachos?

Late August Persian fleet sails to Euboea.

Karystos is forced over to the Persian side.

Siege and fall of Eretria.

1 September? Persian fleet lands at Marathon.

2 September News reaches Athens of the Persian landing at Marathon.

Philippides sets out for Sparta.

3 September Philippides reaches Sparta.

4 September Philippides returns to Athens.

The Athenian assembly accepts the motion of Miltiades 'to set out once they have obtained food' to Marathon. A messenger is sent asking the Plataeans to join them at Marathon.

Night Athenian army sets out for Marathon.

5 September, morning Athenians camp in the Herakleion.

Evening? The Plataeans join the Athenians at Marathon.

6 September? Datis appeals to the Athenians to submit.

The debate of the Athenian generals.

9 September, first light Lakedaimonian advance guard leaves Sparta.

10 September The Persians break camp.

Half the Persian forces including the cavalry embark and put to sea.

Night Ionians inform the Athenians that 'The cavalry is away'.

11 September, morning Battle of Marathon

Evening The Athenian march to the Sanctuary of Herakles at Knynosarges.

12 September Arrival of the Lakedaimonian advance guard at Athens.

Persian fleet leaves Bay of Phaleron and sails to Mykonos.

13 September The Lakedaimonians visit Marathon and inspect the Persian dead.

10 October First sacrifice to Artemis Agroteria celebrating the victory.

October Miltiades leads the expedition against Paros.

Miltiades returns to Athens having failed to take Paros.

November? Trial, imprisonment and death of Miltiades.

Note:

The key chronology which places the battle itself on 11 September (17 *Metageitnion*) is explained on pages 37 and 50 in the text above. The equation of the Athenian months with the months of the contemporary calendar is based on the statement in Herodotus (6.106) that the full moon took place on the 15th day of the second month of the year of Marathon. Astronomical calculation establishes that there was a full moon on 9 September in 490BC. Therefore 15 Metageitnion should correspond to 9 September in 490BC. The Athenian year was divided into 12 lunisolar months of 30 days each (a total of 360 days). The month was divided into three decades of ten days. The seven-day week is a Jewish calendrical system, which only entered the European year much later with the adoption of Christianity. Extra days were intercalated rather haphazardly to keep the calendar in synchronisation with both the phases of the moon and the sun, however, so absolute certainty is not possible. Nevertheless it is improbable that there was a discrepancy so early on in the year. All the other dates offered in this reconstruction are speculative and are extrapolated from my reconstruction of the relative chronology between, and at either side of, the known dates of Philippides departure from Athens and the date of the arrival of the advance party of the Lakedaimonian forces in Athens.

BIBLIOGRAPHY AND SOURCES

Our prime written source for Marathon is Herodotus. Any reconstruction of the battle must be firmly anchored on his account. There is some evidence that he researched the battle carefully. He certainly conducted personal interviews when trying to find out the circumstances surrounding the blinding of Epizelos during the battle, for he (6.117) states: 'I ascertained that Epizelos used to say these things'. Herodotus first recited his *Histories* in Athens in about 425BC (though the date is hotly debated, some place it a decade or so later). At this date Aristophanes was putting on his production of *Acharnians,* which mentions (line 180), that a few veterans of the battle – 'men as hard as oak' – were still alive.

Occasionally Herodotus can be supplemented from a variety of later written sources. The most important is the *Miltiades* of Cornelius Nepos, written around the third quarter of the 1st Century BC. Hammond (1968, 53) suggested that this work and several fragmentary passages gathered in the *Lexicon* of Suidas and in other later sources, might be based on the works of Demon. Demon wrote a local history of Attica and a collection of proverbs in around 300BC. Pausanias' traveller's guide to Greece is also of value. Though written six and a half centuries after the battle, it describes in detail the ancient topography of the Marathon plain. He also records local tradition concerning the battle, some of mixed value.

Even so, there are still significant gaps in our knowledge of what happened at the battle. In an article published in 1964, though first communicated in 1920, Whatley (123–4) pointed out the near impossibility of reconstructing any battle of antiquity, because of the inadequate nature of the written sources. He stressed that the key to arriving at a plausible reconstruction is a thorough investigation of the topography of the battlefield. The art of reconstructing Marathon lies in understanding precisely what Herodotus is saying, and relating his account to the ancient topography of the Marathon plain.

FURTHER READING

A huge amount has been written about Marathon. Every basic handbook on Greek history has an account. The following list includes only works which have been of special help, and which have been referred to more than once in the text.

H.C. Avery, 'Herodotus 6.112.2', *Transactions of the American Philological Association* 103 (1972) 15–22.

H.C. Avery, 'The Number of Persian Dead at Marathon', *Historia* 22 (1973) 757.

E. Badian, 'The Name of the Runner', *American Journal of Ancient History* 4 (1979) 163–6.

A.A. Barrett, M.J. Vickers, 'The Oxford Brygos cup reconsidered', *Journal of Hellenic Studies* 98 (1978) 17–24.

Richard M. Berthold, 'Which Way to Marathon?', *Revue des Études Anciennes* 78/9 (1976/7) 84–95.

P.J. Bicknell, 'The Command Structure and Generals of the Marathon Campaign', *L' Antiquité Classique* 39 (1970) 427–44.

A.R. Burn, 'Thermopylai Revisited and some Topographical Notes on Marathon and Plataiai', *Greece and the Ancient Mediterranean in Ancient History and Prehistory: Studies presented to F. Schachermeyr* ed. K.H. Kinzl (1977) 89–105.

A.R. Burn, *Persia & the Greeks* (1984)

J.A.S. Evans, 'Cavalry About the Time of the Persian Wars: A Speculative Essay', *The Classical Journal* 82 (1987) 97–106.

F. Frost, 'The Dubious Origins of the Marathon', *American Journal of Ancient History* 4 (1979) 159–63.

Robert Garland, *Introducing New Gods. The Politics of Athenian Religion* (1992).

George Grote, *A History of Greece* IV (ed. 1869).

N.G.L. Hammond, 'The Campaign and Battle of Marathon', *Journal of Hellenic Studies* 88 (1968) 13–57.

N.G.L. Hammond, 'Plataea's relations with Thebes, Sparta and Athens', *Journal of Hellenic Studies* 112 (1992) 143–50.

Evelyn B. Harrison, 'The Victory of Kallimachos', *Greek, Roman and Byzantine Studies* 12 (1971) 5–24.

A. Trevor Hodge, 'Marathon: The Persians' Voyage', *Transactions of the American Philological Association* 105 (1975) 95–113.

A. Trevor Hodge, 'Reflections on the shield at Marathon', *Annual of the British School at Athens* 96 (2001) 237–259.

W.W. How and J. Wells, *A Commentary on Herodotus II* (1912)

J.F. Lazenby, *The Defence of Greece 490–479 B.C.* (1993).

D.M. Lewis, 'Datis the Mede' *Journal of Hellenic Studies* 100 (1980) 194–5 H.C.

F. Maurice, 'The Campaign of Marathon', *Journal of Hellenic Studies* 52 (1932) 13–24.

W. McLeod, 'The Bowshot and Marathon', *Journal of Hellenic Studies* 90 (1970) 197–8.

J.A.R. Munro, 'Some Observations on the Persian Wars. 1. – The Campaign of Marathon', *Journal of Hellenic Studies* 19 (1899) 185–97.

Basil Petrakos, *Marathon* (1996).

W.K. Pritchett, 'Marathon', *University of California Publications in Classical Archaeology* 4, no. 2 (1960).

W.K. Pritchett, *Studies in Ancient Greek Topography Part I* (1965).

A. Raubitschek, 'The Gates in the Agora', *American Journal of Archaeology* 60 (1956) 279–82.

A. Raubitschek, 'Das Datisleid', *Charites K. Schauenburg* (1957) 234–42.

P.K. Baillie Reynolds, 'The Shield Signal at the Battle of Marathon', *Journal of Hellenic Studies* 49 (1929) 100–5.

Raphael Sealey, 'The Pit and the Well', *Classical Journal* 72 (1976) 13–20.

I.G. Shrimpton, 'The Persian Cavalry at Marathon', *Phoenix* 34 (1984) 20.

E. Vanderpool, 'A Monument to the Battle of Marathon', *Hesperia* 35 (1966) 93–106.

E. Vanderpool, 'The Deme of Marathon and the Herakleion', *American Journal of Archaeology* 70 (1966) 319–23.

J.A.G. Van Der Veer, 'The Battle of Marathon. A Topographical Survey', *Mnemosyne* 35 (1982) 290–321.

W.P. Wallace, 'Kleomenes, Marathon, the Helots, and Arkadia', *Journal of Hellenic Studies* 74 (1954) 32–5.

N. Whatley, 'On the Possibility of Reconstructing Marathon and Other Ancient Battles', *Journal of Hellenic Studies* 84 (1964) 119–139.

D. Williams, 'A cup by the Antiphon Painter and the Battle of Marathon', in *Studien zur Mythologie und Vasenmalerei Konrad Schauenburg* (Mainz am Rhein 1986) p.75–81.

INDEX

Figures in **bold** refer to illustrations

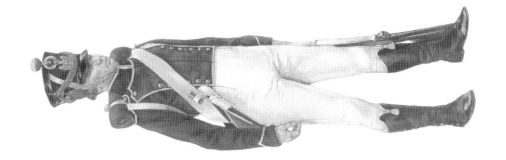 

FIND OUT MORE ABOUT OSPREY

❏ Please send me the latest listing of Osprey's publications

❏ I would like to subscribe to Osprey's e-mail newsletter

Title / rank

Name

Address

City / county

Postcode / zip   state / country

e-mail

CAM

I am interested in:

❏ Ancient world
❏ Medieval world
❏ 16th century
❏ 17th century
❏ 18th century
❏ Napoleonic
❏ 19th century

❏ American Civil War
❏ World War 1
❏ World War 2
❏ Modern warfare
❏ Military aviation
❏ Naval warfare

Please send to:

North America:
Osprey Direct , 2427 Bond Street, University Park, IL 60466, USA

UK, Europe and rest of world:
Osprey Direct UK, P.O. Box 140, Wellingborough, Northants, NN8 2FA, United Kingdom

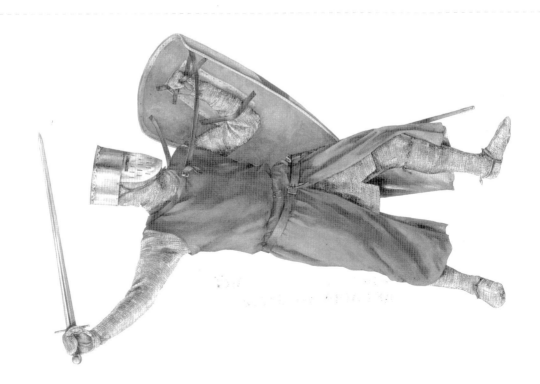

DATE DUE

Demco

www.ospreypublishing.com

call our telephone hotline
for a free information pack

USA & Canada: 1-800-826-6600
UK, Europe and rest of world call:
+44 (0) 1933 443 863

Young Guardsman
Figure taken from *Warrior 22:
Imperial Guardsman 1799–1815*
Published by Osprey
Illustrated by Richard Hook

POSTCARD

Knight, c.1190
Figure taken from *Warrior 1: Norman Knight 950 – 1204 AD*
Published by Osprey
Illustrated by Christa Hook